AF593877

FOR HONOUR ALONE

This book is for Rachel

FOR HONOUR ALONE

The Cadets of Saumur in the Defence of the Cavalry School, France, June 1940

Roy Macnab

ROBERT HALE · LONDON

First published in Great Britain 1988

Robert Hale Limited
Clerkenwell House
Clerkenwell Green
London EC1R 0HT

British Library Cataloguing in Publication Data

Macnab, Roy, *1923–*
For honour alone : the cadets of Saumur
in the defence of the Cavalry School,
1940.
1. World War 2. Military operations by
French military forces. 1939–1940
I. Title.
940.54′13′44

ISBN 0-7090-3331-1

Set in Ehrhardt by Derek Doyle & Associates, Mold, Clwyd.
Printed in Great Britain by
St Edmundsbury Press Ltd, Bury St Edmunds, Suffolk
and bound by WBC Bookbinders Ltd.

Contents

'Yet amid all the adverse accounts from these days of France's expiring agony, one episode at least will always leap forth from French history books in a blaze of glory, the kind of glory belonging almost to a past age. On 19 June, the day Pétain was asking for an armistice, Bock's Panzers had reached Saumur on the Loire, the site of the famous cavalry school. Though still under instruction, the young cadets decided that they would not allow the school to fall without a fight. Armed only with training weapons, they held the Saumur bridges for two whole days against Panzers, until at last their ammunition ran out.'

Alistair Horne, *To Lose a Battle – France 1940*

'On the 19th, between Tours and Saumur, the enemy broke down the last resistance on the river – despite the efforts of the cadets of the cavalry school at Saumur, who on this day wrote a page of glory into French history.'

Colonel A. Goutard, *Fall of France*

Contents

'Yet amid all the adverse accounts from these days of France's expiring agony, one episode at least will always leap forth from French history books in a blaze of glory, the kind of glory belonging almost to a past age. On 19 June, the day Pétain was asking for an armistice, Bock's Panzers had reached Saumur on the Loire, the site of the famous cavalry school. Though still under instruction, the young cadets decided that they would not allow the school to fall without a fight. Armed only with training weapons, they held the Saumur bridges for two whole days against Panzers, until at last their ammunition ran out.'

Alistair Horne, *To Lose a Battle – France 1940*

'On the 19th, between Tours and Saumur, the enemy broke down the last resistance on the river – despite the efforts of the cadets of the cavalry school at Saumur, who on this day wrote a page of glory into French history.'

Colonel A. Goutard, *Fall of France*

List of Illustrations

facing page

Acknowledgements

The story of the Cadets of Saumur of June 1940 and of their heroic defence of the Cavalry School has long been a legend in France but this is the first full account of it in English. In writing it I must record my appreciation of my French predecessors, such writers as Elie Chamard, Pierre Nord, Robert Milliat, Antoine Redier, Colonel Rémy and Maurice Druon of the French Academy. In carrying out my own researches I was helped and encouraged by many people, not least those cadets to whom I put my questions and who, after nearly half a century, recalled for me three days when they made history on the Loire. To one of these I am particularly grateful: Raymond Deutz d' Arragon, now a retired general and President of the *Amicale des Cadets de Saumur et de leurs Compagnons d'armes*, was tireless in his efforts to help me in my task and I am indebted to him for his generous introduction to this book.

Colonel de France, Commandant of the Cavalry School, gave much of his time to take me over the ground and show me where and how it all happened. His archivist, Madame Bouchet, widow of an *Écuyer-en-Chef* of the *Cadre Noir*, and her successor, Madame Garban, found for me the material that I needed. Michelle Audouin-Le Marec, who herself has written about the Saumur of 1940 and the Occupation, gave me the benefit of her own researches and generously allowed me to use the photographs of Instructor Lieutenants Buffévent and Roimarmier and the Desplats armoured car. The late Michel Liffort de Buffévent, brother of one of the fallen heroes of the battle, together with Norbert Bontoux, author of *Île de Gennes*, and Baron Moreau de Bellaing, were others who were very helpful. The artist among the cadets, Geoffroy de Navacelle, has kindly allowed me to use sketches he made at the time.

Another cadet, Roger Stroh, was uniquely helpful. After the war he became a professor of English so he was able to read and correct my text and convey its contents to his colleagues.

Acknowledgement is due to the *École d'Application de l'Arme Blindée et de la Cavalerie* (*EAABC*), as the Cavalry School is now known, for providing most of my illustrations; to the *École Nationale d'Equitation* for photographs of the *Cadre Noir* and, in particular, to its former *Écuyer-en-Chef*, Colonel Durand; to the *Bundesarchiv* at Koblenz for the photograph of General Feldt; to the *Service Historique de l'Armée* at Vincennes for allowing me to see official records such as the reports by General Pichon and Colonel Michon; to the tourist office of Saumur; Mlle M.T. Pessonnier of Saumur, and to Andrew Lanham who were particularly helpful in securing and providing photographs.

I am specially grateful to Alistair Horne, author of the standard work *To Lose a Battle: France 1940*, not only for his advice and guidance but for allowing me to reproduce a paragraph from his book as a frontispiece for mine. Acknowledgement for other extracts from copyright material is made to Ambassador Hervé Alphand (*Etonnement d'être*); Eyre and Spottiswoode for P. Baudouin's *Private Diaries*; Macmillan Publishers for General Beaufre's *1940: The Fall of France*; Collins publishers for General de Gaulle's *The Call to Honour, 1940–42*; Macdonald & Co Ltd. for General von Senger und Etterlin's *Neither Fear Nor Hope*; William Heinemann Ltd. for General Weygand's *Recalled to Service*; and to the Bodley Head for André Maurois' *Why France Fell.*

Roy Macnab
Le Lavandou

Foreword

by General R. Deutz d'Arragon, *Président d'Amicale des Cadets de Saumur et leurs Compagnons d'armes*

Some forty-eight years after it all happened, the battles along the Loire in which the Cavalry School at Saumur confronted two divisions of the Germany army on 19, 20, and 21 June 1940, come alive once again in Roy Macnab's account of them.

The defence of the Loire crossings between Montsoreau and Le Thoureil, whose keenest actions took place at Saumur itself, at Gennes and around Aunis Farm, has been the subject of several books in France but this is the first account in English. But is the interest that is still aroused by this episode, in itself just a minor feature of the 1940 drama of the Battle of France, due purely to a heroism so out of the ordinary as to be almost legendary? No, what distinguishes and gives exemplary value to the conduct of the Cadets of Saumur are the peculiar circumstances of their combat and the atmosphere surrounding it.

A military academy prepares its pupils for war; on the other hand, it is not itself called upon to fight. Student officers still under training, weaponry well nigh obsolete and so excessively used as to have become worn-out, communications unserviceable, support non-existent – all these combined to justify the order to the Cavalry School to evacuate to the South of France. That the School, instead, found itself in the firing line was due to the implacable will of its Commandant, Colonel Michon, and to the elevated ideas he had about the honour of the historic school that had been entrusted to him.

Moreover, by the time the German troops reached the Loire,

the fate of our forces had already been sealed as a result of the Germans having got across the Seine in strength. Nothing could now stop the *Wehrmacht's* victorious progress nor delay the conclusion of an armistice that in fact had been requested on 17 June. In such circumstances as these how should one explain the reaction of the cadets who, to a man, were one with their Commandant in his decision to fight?

Roy Macnab, as historian and analyist, has sought an answer by placing these 1940 battles in their geographical and historical context. The Valley of the Loire, that garden of France that was the tarrying-place of French kings – the Cavalry School, descendant of the schools of Versailles and Saint-Germain and since 1814 established at Saumur, where generation after generation of our finest instructors instilled in their young charges the 'cavalier spirit' that is made up of an elegance both physical and of the spirit, of panache and selflessness – love of country, military tradition, self-denial – here are the answers.

In their refusal to accept the inevitable, the officers and pupils of the Cavalry School cannot be dissociated from all those who, of their own free will or under orders, fought alongside them: isolated individuals whose spirit had been severely tested, Algerian riflemen, detachments reformed from survivors of earlier battles, such as Captain de Neuchèze's *Groupe Franc* but, above all, the battalion of infantry cadets from the school at Saint-Maixent who excelled themselves on the plateau of Aunis Farm.

Finally, in addressing an English-speaking public, it is perhaps useful to remind the courageous British people, who were then about to face, on their own, the most critical period in their history, that, shortly before, a handful of young Frenchmen paid their share of the price in 'blood, sweat and tears' so that the national identity of each of our countries might be preserved.

Raymond Deutz d'Arragon

Prologue

At six o'clock on the evening of 18 June 1940, General de Gaulle was broadcasting from a BBC studio in London his historic appeal to his countrymen not to abandon the war against Germany, despite the demand for an armistice that had just been made by the French Government, now under Marshal Pétain. At the same hour a handful of young men on the banks of the Loire, at Saumur, were preparing to sacrifice their lives in a desperate effort to resist the approaching German Panzers. As they saw it, it was to be an action to save the honour of France in the hour of its national humiliation and degradation. They were the Cadets of Saumur, some 780 pupils of France's historic Cavalry School – the *École de Cavalerie*, whose celebrated Black Squadron of military horsemen, the *Cadre Noir*, had won for France in international riding events a prestige equalled only by that of the Spanish Riding Academy of Vienna.

For more than 150 years, the month of June has been the time when Saumur prepares for its annual Carrousel,* when the *Cadre Noir* performs its magic feats of horsemanship in front of the Cavalry School, watched by crowds drawn by its prowess from all parts of the world. That month, in 1940, the Carrousel took a different though now less spectacular form, when the almost medieval qualities of chivalry, of honour and sacrifice, with which the cult of the horse and the tradition of cavalry have long been associated, were demonstrated not in the usual equestrian ballet of *courbette, croupade* and *cabriole* but in bloody and desperate battle and in acts of extraordinary courage and endurance.

* Carrousel: a military tournament with games and allegorical representations. Originally a tilting match for knights on horseback, it developed at Saumur into an elaborate display of equestrian skills.

From midnight on 18 June 1940 until early on 21 June, during some forty-eight hours, a German Panzer division of 18,000 men was held up at Saumur along a 40-kilometre stretch of the Loire on either side of the Cavalry School being defended by its Commandant.

To do this he had just over 2,000 men. They included not only his cadets and their instructors but also scattered remnants of France's broken armies who in the retreat to the south had reached the Cavalry School at Saumur. Among those who came to support the cadets in their stand were survivors of Dunkirk, who, having been lifted from the beaches by the Royal Navy and French fleet, had been taken to Britain and then made their way back to France in the hope of continuing the struggle.

In later years General de Gaulle was to refer to the sacrifice of the Cadets of Saumur during France's expiring agony in June 1940 as the first act of the Resistance, and when the time came to build the memorial to the Resistance at Mont Valérien in Paris, he insisted that the defence of their Cavalry School by its young cadets should be properly commemorated there.

None of the survivors ever remembered hearing de Gaulle's stirring radio message from London; many had barely heard of de Gaulle. It was not that broadcast of 18 June that had stirred them, though they acted within its spirit, but that made by Marshal Pétain on the previous day. And that had driven them to anger and dismay, as, in the mess over lunch, they had listened to the thin, pathetic voice of their new Prime Minister, the eighty-four-year-old Marshal of France, telling them that the war was lost, that they must lay down their arms, that he was seeking an armistice with the Germans. It was a mockery of everything that Saumur had taught its cadets: to surrender without fighting was unthinkable; that, too, was the view of the Commandant of the Cavalry School and of the young, aristocratic officers who were their instructors.

Meanwhile, about seventy kilometres away, up river from Saumur, at Tours, where only a few days earlier Britain's Prime Minister Winston Churchill, had made a last personal effort to keep France in the war, the French armistice convoy followed Hitler's instructions and crossed the Loire into the German lines. Then it continued northward along the crowded roads to Paris and beyond to Compiègne for the final act of France's disgrace, when, in the clearing at Réthondes, in the same railway carriage where the 1918 armistice had been signed, Hitler himself was present to see his surrender terms handed to the French delegation.

While France and Germany were going through this ritual that would bring hostilities between them officially to an end, the Cadets of Saumur, still under training and never having heard a shot fired in anger, armed with outdated weapons, including a gun from the School museum, fought their hopeless but glorious battle. In the event, it was not a gesture devoid of military value for, by holding the Germans on the Loire for two days, they enabled the entire 200,000-strong Army of Paris, retreating to the east of them, to evade capture and reach the safety of the Unoccupied Zone before the armistice was signed.

In the widespread chaos of June 1940, when not only were France's armies in headlong retreat but millions of its ordinary citizens, who had quit their homes and taken to the roads before the German advance, the combat at Saumur was a battle out of its time, barely related to what was happening elsewhere in France, conducted almost in the manner of a tournament by each of the adversaries. The challenge made by the Cadets of Saumur, most of them still in their teens, was not to just any unit of the German Army but, though they did not know it at first, to the German cavalry itself.

By pure coincidence, the German advance guard that reached the Loire at midnight on the 18 June 1940 was the 1st Cavalry Division of the Wehrmacht, whose officers were products of Germany's equivalent of Saumur, the cavalry school at Hanover. Like the instructors and cadets of Saumur, their officers came from aristocratic families with military traditions; unlike the Cadets of Saumur they were already seasoned warriors, having taken part with great distinction in the Polish campaign as mounted troops. At Saumur, however, they arrived as motorized cavalrymen but the French cavalry cadets had no horses either. A few hours before the battle began a convoy of some 800 horses left Saumur along the road to the South. It was led by one of France's most celebrated international riders, an officer of the *Cadre Noir*, who had in his convoy the country's leading competitors in international events including the champion of the 1932 Olympic Games.

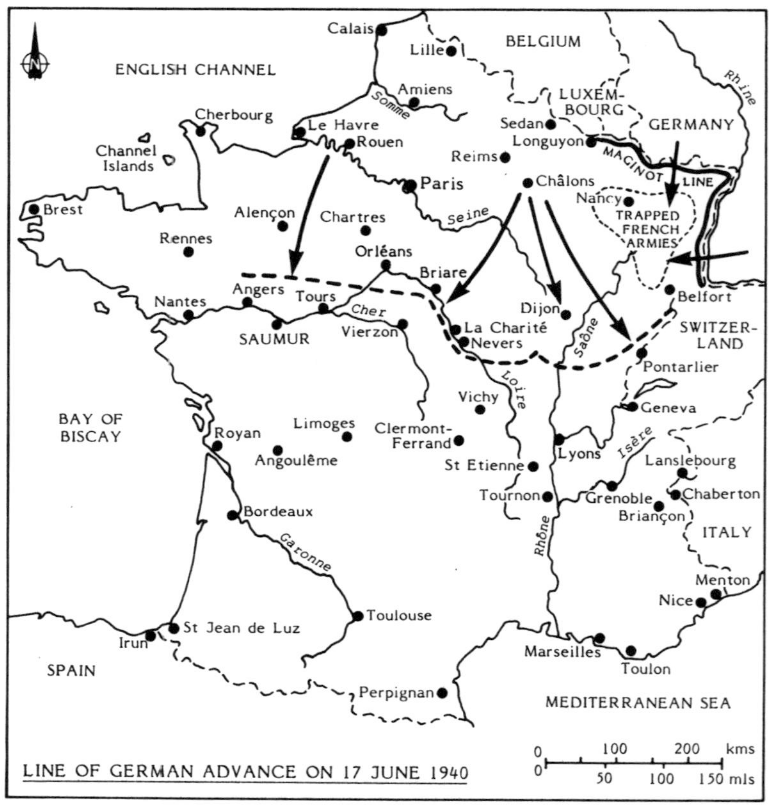

It was indicative of the spirit in which the Saumur combat was conducted that when, in a few days, cadets, horses, the Cavalry School itself, were in German hands, the German general, moved by the courage of the young cadets who had fought until their ammunition had run out, behaved with a kind of chivalry both towards the cadets and the horses of the *Cadre Noir*, rarely seen in times of modern warfare.

The German Press, reporting on the bravery of the young men of Saumur, referred to them as 'cadets', a word that had not been used since the Revolution. It is still not used except to describe those who in June 1940 took part in the combat at Saumur, where today one of the bridges into the town bears the name 'Pont des Cadets de Saumur', and where along the river are scattered memorials and gravestones that recall poignantly the sacrifice of a young French élite who could not accept the disgrace of their country's surrender.

Despite its theatrical overtones, recalling the cadets of Gascogne in the battle of Arras in Edmond Rostand's play *Cyrano de Bergerac* the combat at Saumur presented a moral problem that belonged to the real world of 1940 – as was forcibly illustrated by the agonizing exchanges between a young officer and a priest at the height of the battle.

There was, however, another conversation that always comes to mind when each year the crowds reassemble at the Cavalry School at Saumur to watch the *Cadre Noir* perform their Carrousel, the words of a cadet and those of his instructor lieutenant. They could have come straight out of *Cyrano de Bergerac*.

Cadet: *'Mon Lieutenant, c'est à la mort que vous m'envoyez.'*

Instructor: *'Je vous fait cet honneur, Monsieur.'*

'You are sending me to my death,' the cadet had said, and his lieutenant had replied magnificently, 'I do you that honour, sir.' Cadet and instructor survived as France survived and four years later, with the Allied armies in Italy, the instructor was awarded the DSO by King George VI, the citation referring to him as a 'magnificent leader and brilliant commander of men'. Many years later as a general he received one of the highest honours that can be bestowed upon a French soldier, the Governorship of Les Invalides in Paris. On a wall at Les Invalides, in its *Cour d'Honneur*, not far from the tomb of Napoleon, there is a plaque. On it are the words taken from another citation, that issued by the French Army to honour the Cadets of Saumur of June 1940. The words of this citation, like those used by the Governor of Les Invalides as a twenty-eight-year-old instructor at Saumur in 1940, have found their way into France's histories of the period as indicating the kind of spirit that was still alive in the France of June 1940, despite everything that had happened and was about to happen as the long calvary of the German occupation began.

And if the Cadets of Saumur came to be regarded as the first heroes of the Resistance, it was also appropriate that some of the heroes of the Liberation in 1944 should also be the sons of the Cavalry School of Saumur. Two of them became Marshals of France, a third, who actually liberated his old *alma mater* on 30 August 1944, was perhaps the most remarkable of them all since he was not a Frenchman but an American.

What follows, then, is the story of the Cadets of Saumur of June 1940. It is also an attempt to explain the existence at that time of two Frances, very different each from the other when the moment of truth came: a France divided against itself, a France of quarrelling and indecisive political leaders, of old and defeatist generals incapable of dealing with the new kind of warfare, the *Blitzkrieg*, launched by the German armies against them in May 1940; and another France, survival of a romantic past, seemingly unaware of the real world of 1940, characterized by the military-monasticism of the Cavalry School of Saumur. Here was the *'France éternelle'* of General de Gaulle of whose ancient values he was speaking from London at that time of crisis and for which the Cadets of Saumur performed their extraordinary if tragic Carrousel, thereby finding a place not only in the history but among the legends of their country.

1 Ancestors and Atavism

If the conduct of the young Cadets of Saumur in June 1940 seems to have belonged to a different age, it is perhaps because so little has changed in the beautiful and romantic landscape of Anjou, in the valley of the slowly flowing Loire, since its great fortresses were built in the Middle Ages, and its châteaux during the Renaissance.

In the Abbey of Fontevrault, some three kilometres behind the stretch of the Loire defended by the cadets, are the tombs and effigies of the English king Henry II and his wife Eleanor of Aquitaine; their son, Richard Cœur de Lion; their daughter-in-law Isabella, the second wife of King John. It was here that Colonel du Vigier, bringing his men back from Britain after Dunkirk, regrouped them to continue the fight alongside the cadets, who themselves, when the battle for the school was over, took refuge in the forest and were captured there.

It is almost as if there were something in the soil of western France to fertilize heroic legend. So much of France's history has taken place along this great river, the longest in France, its thousand kilometres of water rising in the high country of the Auvergne, running north and then turning westward towards the borders of Brittany and the sea, and in so doing it seems to divide France in two, the north from the south. Even the climate seems to change on crossing the Loire: going south there is the prospect of sunshine and the Mediterranean warmth of Provence whose masters were also at one time dukes of Anjou. The province of Anjou has 125 miles of the Loire to itself. The town of Saumur, whose great fairy-tale château on the heights has looked down, since 1763, on the Cavalry School below, lies with the town of Angers to its west and Tours to its east.

It is a smiling country of vineyards, orchards and neat

farmhouses, surrounded by vegetable gardens, and with the clear skies and bright sunshine of June days, it has an almost Arcadian atmosphere of pastoral peace. But the smile and the peace are deceptive, for over the centuries this valley of the Loire has frequently been a battlefield, as often as not with Englishmen and Frenchmen in opposing armies. In the fourteenth and fifteenth centuries they fought the Hundred Years War, which in its later stages introduced to the Loire one of the great figures of French mythology, Joan of Arc, who lifted the English siege at Orleans in 1429 and at Chinon inspired the Dauphin to ascend the throne of France as Charles VII.

St Joan of Arc was, of course, Joan of Lorraine, and it was the Cross of Lorraine, with its distinctive shorter cross-bar above the normal one, that General de Gaulle, in London in 1940, took as the banner of his Free French forces and which, in stone, dominates the countryside for miles around his grave at his old home at Colombey-les-deux-églises. But the Cross of Lorraine is really the Cross of Anjou, the dukes of Lorraine having adopted it as their banner only in the seventeenth century. And the Cross of Anjou, reputedly made from a piece of the True Cross, is still to be found in the church at Baugé, across the river from Saumur.

In the sixteenth century the Loire valley was again a battlefield, this time for France's wars of religion, when Catholic and Protestant opposed each other in bitter battles. From these wars emerged the great figure of Henry of Navarre, who, as Henry IV, produced the Edict of Nantes, which in 1598 gave to Protestant France the religious toleration that it had been seeking. Henry of Navarre lived for a long time at Saumur, and when he finally departed with his army for Paris, he left his friend Duplessis-Mornay, sometimes called 'the Protestant Pope', as Governor there. Saumur soon developed a strong Protestant tradition, Duplessis-Mornay founding there a Protestant university to which was attached a riding school, and these attracted pupils from such Protestant countries as England and Holland. The Revocation of the Edict of Nantes in 1685, however, brought this to an end, and many of the citizens of Saumur were among the quarter of a million Protestants – the Huguenots – who left France to live in England and elsewhere.

In another hundred years Frenchmen were again fighting

each other along the Loire, following the revolution of 1789, when western France, notably the Vendée, continued to fight for the Royalist cause long after it had been lost to the revolutionaries elsewhere. At Bressuire, on the road south from Saumur, the twenty-one-year-old hero of the Royalist resistance 'Monsieur Henri' – Henri de la Rochejacquelin – rallied his men with the cry: 'If I advance, follow me. If I retreat, kill me. If I die, avenge me!' These were words which at Bressuire, at exactly the same place on 21 June 1940, were to have an echo among others of his tender age.

In 1832 the Duchess of Berry, in whose presence the first Carrousel ever staged at the Cavalry School was held four years earlier, disturbed the peace of western France when she tried unsuccessfully to raise a Royalist rebellion in the name of her son, the Bourbon Pretender.

Another forty years went by and they were fighting again along the Loire: this time, as in 1940, France was fighting the closing battles of a war against Germany. On the Loire at Blois in 1871, as at Saumur in 1940, young Frenchmen were fighting heroically while their Government was at the armistice table. In June 1940 it was Hitler in the railway coach at Compiègne; in January 1871 it had been the Kaiser in the Hall of Mirrors at Versailles – each gave his terms for peace to the delegates of a defeated France.

If the romantic landscape marked with medieval fortresses, and of which the Cavalry School of Saumur forms a part, seems almost to have been overburdened with the history of battles by the Angevin centuries, there are other influences, no less inspiring of patriotism for being less violent, that have helped create the atmosphere in which a young French élite at Saumur has for so long been educated. The Loire is the centre of another tradition, that of literature and in particular poetry.

Although today many memorial stones indicate the place of ancient battles and the feats of past heroes, others mark the homes of Pierre Ronsard, France's great poet of the sixteenth century, of Alfred de Vigny, whose nineteenth-century verses showed so much understanding for the military profession, and of Charles Péguy, soldier-poet of our own century, killed in action on the Marne in 1914. And they recall such great names as Rabelais and Descartes, Balzac and Georges Sand, who belonged to this particular piece of France, poets, prose-writers, philosophers, who in their totality express so much of the spirit of France and to whose influence every Frenchman is exposed at an early age. The Loire valley and its surroundings evoke, therefore, not only the memory of warriors and horsemen but much that is at the heart of France's civilization, nourished at royal courts along the Loire. Francis I provided a home at Amboise for Leonardo da Vinci, and a century earlier there was that attractive and amiable poet-king, René of Anjou, whose daughter Marguerite married England's King Henry VI, founder of Eton and King's College, Cambridge.

Today René the Good is remembered for the famous Apocalypse tapestries which bring the world in admiration to his old home, the castle of Anjou, whose great size and forbidding appearance, with its seventeen towers, dominate the town. But the château of Saumur was also his home; he added greatly to the building that had been erected a century earlier, and he called it 'The Castle of Love'. On Offard Island, in the middle of the river opposite his castle, a notable square bears his name, the Place du Roi René, and nearby is the house where his mother, the Queen of Sicily, lived. It is intact still, having miraculously survived the battle that took place all about it in June 1940, when the cadets defended the island bridge that now bears their name. It was, historically, an appropriate place for them to do so, since the fore-runner of their riding school had been transferred to Saumur from the Château de Pignerolles near King René's castle at Angers. Pignerolles had been built as an exact replica of the Petit Trianon at Versailles and preserved much of the charm that had made the original the beloved possession of Marie Antoinette.

Throughout the eighteenth century the riding school at Pignerolles enjoyed an international reputation, and for young men of good family it was an essential part of their education. Hence, in 1785 to Angers came a seventeen-year-old Irish aristocrat not long out of Eton, to perfect his horsemanship. His name was Arthur Wesley (later Wellesley). Two years later he gained a commission in the British Army in India and in due course he became Field-Marshal the Duke of Wellington. Two other British Prime Ministers who as young men had perfected their riding at this same school were the Earl of Chatham

(William Pitt the Elder) and George Canning.

The riding school was in due course transferred to Saumur, which established itself as the country's most important equestrian centre.

Although young English gentlemen, particularly those who were going into the cavalry, would spend some time in France's riding schools, many of their French riding instructors had been influenced in their teaching by a manual on how to train horses and riders written by the first Duke of Newcastle. The Duke, a favourite of Charles II, had been a distinguished Royalist general in the Civil War. He was also a playwright. A refugee in France from Cromwell's England, he had passed his time running a riding school at Angers and in 1658, after his manual had been translated into French by Monsieur de Solleysel, the Newcastle methods became part of the basic procedures wherever Frenchmen were training horses and cavalry. And as such he became in due course part of the Saumur tradition.

In 1911 the veterinary surgeon at the Cavalry School, Monsieur Joly, founded the *Musée du Cheval*, the Horse Museum, on an upper floor of the château of Saumur, and thereafter pupil officers at the Cavalry School were taught here the long and fascinating history of horses and horsemanship at Saumur and how often this had been laced with English influences. These go back to Richard Cœur de Lion, the first monarch to introduce Arab horses to England, whence in due course the French imported thoroughbred sires to build up their own stud. Here in Joly's museum at Saumur is the skeleton of Flying Fox, which in 1899 won every important British race, including the Derby. Sold to France by the executors of the first Duke of Westminster, Flying Fox became the founder of a dynasty of French thoroughbreds, the pride of Saumur.

Saumur's reputation for horses and horsemanship was already long established by the time the *École de Cavalerie* was founded in 1763. In that year a brigade of carabineers was sent to garrison Saumur. They were picked troops, known as the Royal Carabineers of Monsieur – 'Monsieur' being the informal title of the King's brother, the Count of Provence, who was colonel of the regiment. Lacking proper accommodation, they were at first quartered on the townsfolk, who looked upon their arrival with some disquiet. However, work soon began on their barracks, stables and riding school. All these together form the present Cavalry School in front of which is the great open space known as the Chardonnet which runs down to the banks of the Loire. It is so named because of the thistles *(chardons)* that used to grow there in the dry season. The Chardonnet has been used for riding events since the eleventh century, when knights in armour jousted there, and in the Carrousel of today there are echoes still of those times.

After the arrival of the Carabineers of Monsieur, the Cavalry School evolved rapidly under the influence of the Duke of Choiseul, the war minister who reorganized the army after the poor performance of the cavalry in the Seven Years War (1742-8). At that time the Army was run largely by private enterprise, with particular individuals commanding their own companies which they financed and maintained. Choiseul decided that all troops should be the King's responsibility to maintain and that the State should provide all the horses for the cavalry. At the same time he established a number of cavalry schools about the country in the hope of improving the standard of military horsemanship. In 1776, on a tour of inspection of these schools, he was particularly impressed by the methods of instruction and the general efficiency of Saumur under its Commandant, the Marquis de Poyanne. As a result he called a meeting in Paris of his cavalry inspectors and colonels, when it was decided to apply the Saumur methods generally throughout the country. It was not long, however, before the *École de Cavalerie* became the only centre for cavalry training in France, and from then on all cavalry regiments had to send to Saumur officers specially selected for training there. In this way the Saumur tradition was established.

That tradition was broken temporarily during the Revolution and in Napoleon's time, when the Emperor opened his own school at St-Germain, but it re-emerged in 1814, thanks to Marshal Soult, the War Minister, and except for a break between 1822 and 1825, when it was closed, it has functioned ever since. In 1825 the Commandant of the School, General Oudinot, imported horses from Ireland and saddles from England. He transmitted his enthusiasm for horsemanship to everyone who came under his command, and it was on his initiative that the first Carrousel was organized for the visit to

Saumur of the Duchess of Berry in 1828.

The riding instructors were given the name *écuyer*, equerry, which they still enjoy, although almost from the beginning the young pupil officers would refer to them as 'the gods' since they considered the *manège* (riding school) to be like Olympus. The *écuyers* formed the *Cadre Noir*, so named because of their black uniforms, which progressed from frock coat to short jacket to split tunic. In full dress uniform they still wear the traditional two-cornered hat once worn by all riding pupils in the school and known as a *'lampion'* (lantern). Their everyday uniform as they went about their duties at Saumur, the black habit suggestive of the military monk, was relieved only by the gold stripes of rank, by their buttons and by the shining metal of their spurs. The *Écuyer-en-Chef*, often a French horseman of international reputation, was of colonel's rank and assisted by some ten other officers of varying rank, all selected from cavalry regiments and detached for full-time duties at Saumur.

Other instructors at the Cavalry School – that is, other than the riding instructors – wear the traditional blue uniform of the French Army and are known as the *Cadre Bleu*.

'Horsemanship is not everything in the Cavalry,' wrote Marshal Soult in a message to the school in 1840, 'but everything is nothing without it.' Exactly 100 years later there were not a few of the young cadets of Saumur who still believed this and who, on arriving for training in April, 1940, were more excited at the prospect of riding some of the finest horses in France than of operating the tanks and armoured cars that had overtaken the horse as the vehicle of modern cavalry.

It was the combination of Cavalry School and riding school – of *Cadre Bleu* and *Cadre Noir* – that made Saumur different from other great equestrian centres, that of the Spanish Academy of Vienna, for instance, or the old Royal Riding School of Versailles. There were times when the prestige of the riding school almost eclipsed that of the Cavalry School of which it was a part. One of Saumur's great figures, General l'Hotte, wrote during the nineteenth century that he sometimes wondered if the *Écuyer-en-Chef* enjoyed a more important position than the Commandant of the Cavalry School. 'I can express this opinion as I held both positions,' he said.

The Carrousel dramatized every year the glamour of the

Cadre Noir and impressed itself forcibly on generation after generation of young men who came to Saumur, usually after completing their elementary studies at St-Cyr, in order to qualify for a commission in the cavalry. The only time when the Carrousel has not been held has been when France has been at war – in 1870, for instance, and during the two World Wars. In 1914 France's call for mobilization came right in the middle of the Carrousel.

It was these wars and earlier campaigns and the military leaders they produced that contributed to the celebrity of the *École de Cavalerie* beside whose great stone staircase of honour are inscribed on marble slabs the names of those Marshals of France who were cavalrymen, of French Generals of the Cavalry who died in action, and of Commandants of the school over the centuries. At Saumur one encounters such names as Foch, Marshal of France and British Field-Marshal, of Marshal Lyautey and that enigmatic figure General Weygand, who had been pupil and Chief Instructor, head of the *Cadre Bleu* at Saumur, who played such a controversial role as Commander-in-Chief when France fell in June 1940, who signed the Army's citation on the Cadets of Saumur and who in 1965, at the age of ninety-eight, was still able to send a message of exhortation to a new generation of young cavalry officers-in-the-making.

After the First World War, which had seen the emergence of the era of mechanized warfare, the Cavalry School at Saumur became increasingly concerned with these new conditions. But the horse, if no longer a suitable companion in battle, found a new role at Saumur. Breaking in and training horses were still thought to be useful aids to the training of soldierly qualities in young pupil officers, even in a mechanical age, and the growing popularity of international riding events in the post-war world and the prestige won by national teams in world competition prompted Saumur to create its own special centre for the training of officers for these competitions. The centre was opened in 1922, with Colonel Haentjens in command, and in due course he was succeeded by Colonel de Laissardière, who, together with such junior officers as Bizard, Durand and de Castres,* became popular and successful personalities in the

* De Castres, who held the world record for the highest jump on horseback,

international events of the 1930s, at Wembley in London where de Laissardière in three separate years won the Prince of Wales prize, at Geneva, Brussels and, ironically, Berlin, in February 1939 on the eve of war, when they got to know some of the German cavalry riders who in June the following year were to do battle with them in earnest on the banks of the Loire at Saumur. And, as will be seen, Colonel de Laissardière's reputation as an international champion was to stand him in good stead when, having led away his 800 horses from Saumur in June 1940, he had to entreat his German captors for their release.

By 1939 the riding school had put the *École de Cavalerie* very much on the map internationally; the uniform of the *Cadre Noir* had become familiar to spectators in many parts of the world; their own panache was matched by that of their horses, harnessed in gold and purple and with their manes plaited with silk ribbon. The French success at the Olympic Games at Los Angeles in 1932, with Commandant Lesage riding Taine, ensured that every year at the Carrousel at Saumur an international audience would pack the stands erected in front of the school.

Riding activities were not confined to show-jumping or the particular ballet-like movements of the *'sauters en liberté'*, horses specially trained to respond to the curious incantation of their riders to do the *courbette, croupade* or *cabriole*, performances of precision and control normally seen only in circus animals. The steeplechase – the same term is used in France – and polo also became popular pastimes among the young cavalrymen at Saumur. As early as 1850 military races were being held on the nearby course at Breil; at Verrie and at Varrains, too, military races were held regularly. International civilian teams competed with the *Cadre Noir* at polo on the Breil ground. In the 1930s France was not lacking in competitive skills: as Guy Chapman pointed out in his book *The Collapse of France*, 'The test pilots at Villacoublay like the famous *Cadre Noir* of the Saumur Cavalry School were so skilled that they could do anything.'

As the 1930s progressed and while Germany, under Hitler,

---

was to achieve lasting fame as a general, the defender of Dien Bien Phu in Indo-China in 1954; he died in 1984.

was re-arming to create the Panzers of its mechanized fighting force, France might sometimes have given the impression of being over-content with the past, and Saumur, with its black riders performing on the Chardonnet, no doubt contributed to that impression. As Chapman said of the French Army: 'They had accepted but not welcomed the armoured fighting vehicle. The training establishments St-Cyr, Polytechnique, Saumur, *École Supérieure de Guerre, Centre des Hautes Études Militaires*, considered it in no way revolutionary or necessary and continued to treat it as an outsider as well as a *parvenu*.'

There was one French officer who did not take this view. In 1934 he wrote a book which he called *Vers l'Armée de Métier* (*Towards a Professional Army*) in which he made an eloquent plea for France to equip its army to fight the war of the future, which would be a war of machines, of armoured vehicles in particular. 'As to the cavalry,' he wrote, 'powerless to cover broken ground, badly equipped for combat, infinitely vulnerable, its dream of horsemanship shattered at the first complication, beaten by machine-guns.' This far-seeing officer, a colonel who had fought in the First World War, was Charles de Gaulle, who was trying to persuade Parliamentarians and members of the Government to provide France with 3,000 modern tanks and six armoured divisions. Some years earlier, General Weygand, whose career had been so intimately connected with Saumur and its Cavalry School, had written: 'War in the future even more than in the last war will be a war of machines – may the cavalry approach the machine in the belief that it will not replace cavalry but give it additional power, that it is not a rival but a friend.'

This approach had been adopted at Saumur, where, despite the glamorous influence of the *Cadre Noir*, the Cavalry School was turning increasingly to the serious military business of tanks and armoured cars and other forms of motorized cavalry. Training centres in the use of armoured vehicles were set up not far off at Fontevrault and at Angers. Moreover, in 1928 the Cavalry School was reorganized to cater also for the education of pupil officers for the *Train* – the Army Service Corps. At first sight Cavalry and Service Corps might seem odd bedfellows, since the latter is not a fighting unit, but transport, originally horse-drawn and later motorized, provided the common factor.

And when, in June 1940, the time came for the cadets to defend the school, the young Service Corps pupils fought with the same determination as their comrades of the Cavalry.

On the first day of mobilization in France, 21 August 1939, all the military instructors at Saumur, the *Cadre Bleu* together with their pupils who had completed their course, departed to join the units to which they had been assigned. The *écuyers* of the *Cadre Noir*, too, bade goodbye to their horses and for the most part took command of motorized units. Some 600 horses from the school left for service with the twenty-five units still using horses. This compared with the eighty-five regiments of cavalry from which the *Cadre Noir* chose its members before the outbreak of the First World War in 1914.

In the early days of the Second World War, after mobilization, the Cavalry School had a somewhat deserted appearance. The former Commandant himself, General Bridoux, had departed to take up an active service appointment and to join his two predecessors, General Petiet and General de la Laurencie. In 1935 General de la Laurencie had published a history of the Cavalry School while serving as its Commandant, and in the battle for France in 1940 he was one of the few French general officers who aroused the admiration of the British ally, when he worked closely with the British Expeditionary Force under General Lord Gort VC.

General Bridoux was replaced as Saumur's Commandant by Colonel Daniel Michon. An old warrior who had first seen action while serving under Marshal Lyautey in Morocco in the early years of the century, he had been severely wounded in the trenches in France during the First World War, and his wounds troubled him still in 1940. At first he had expected to run the school almost on a care-and-maintenance basis. No one at that stage foresaw the long months of the *Drôle de Guerre* – the Phoney War – when the French sat tight behind their Maginot Line and the Germans did the same behind their Siegfried Line. In due course, as will be seen, Colonel Michon was able to resume the traditional role of the Cavalry School and to retrieve from the front line specially selected officers to form his staff of cavalry instructors.

In April the pupils arrived, the Class of 1940 which was to achieve immortality in the annals of the school as 'The Cadets of

Saumur'. Up till that point Colonel Michon had had to provide accommodation for a variety of military groups requiring quick training courses: some were young men straight out of St-Cyr on their way to join regiments at the front; some were non-commissioned officers from the regular army on crash courses on armoured vehicled; finally these were pupil officers of the Reserve. These courses had started in 1935 when a new rank had been introduced, that of *aspirant* – equating the rank of ensign in the Army, midshipman in the Navy. After the outbreak of war, the quickest way for a young man to become a cavalry officer was to be selected as an *élève aspirant de réserve*, known as an EAR, a pupil officer of the Reserve. Not all of them, however, at that stage had chosen the Army as a career: many had already started training for other professions, including the Church, but had volunteered to train as cavalry officers of the Reserve and in open competition had been selected for Saumur.

More than 700 EARs, mostly in their teens, arrived at the Cavalry School in April 1940, almost exclusively from the same social background. Many of those who survived the fighting in June 1940 did become professional soldiers, and among them were those who in due course reached general's rank. But in June 1940 they were amateur soldiers and were still under training. It was a measure of the atmosphere of Saumur itself, and of the quality of leadership of the young lieutenants, still in their twenties, whom Colonel Michon had had sent back from the front to be their instructors for three months, that the cadets acquitted themselves in the way they did in the extraordinary circumstances of France's national crisis in June 1940.

Colonel Michon knew personally each of the twelve instructor lieutenants he had asked for by name to be sent back to Saumur from the front. Each had distinguished himself as a pupil officer on courses over the previous four years. Returning to the peaceful surroundings of Saumur, exchanging the rude regimental life at the front for the civilized surroundings of the Cavalry School hundreds of miles to the south, was not their idea of military service. Most of them, Colonel Michon noted, arrived with long faces, but he added: 'In them I have the best soldiers at the front.' However, as one of them, Gérard Liffort de Buffévent, was to say later when with his cadets he had set up his defence position in the Square of King René on Offard

Island to await the arrival of the Germans at the Saumur bridges – 'If I could not go to the war, at least it has now come to me.'

When in due course the Phoney War ended and on 10 May 1940 Germany launched its great offensive with 136 divisions against the Low Countries and France itself, it was perhaps appropriate that the first refugees from the fighting in the north to arrive at Saumur should have been horses.

On 16 May, ten days after the fighting began, officers and their pupils at Saumur, as well as civilians in the streets, witnessed an unexpected spectacle. At four o'clock that afternoon a special train of thirty trucks pulled into the station. It had come from Brussels and had brought to Saumur the entire stables of the King of the Belgians. Through the streets of Saumur on its way to the Cavalry School went all the royal carriages, together with King Leopold's own horse and the Shetland ponies of the heir, Prince Baudouin, and his brother and sisters. They made a splendid sight as they went by in procession. Saumur, everyone believed, was a place of safety; here the horses of the Belgian royal family could be cared for until peace returned.

Not even the grave news that was coming to them of what had been happening that day and the day before at Sedan and on the Meuse could disturb the confidence, that atmosphere of there's-nothing-to-worry-about still everywhere apparent in France, and not least at Saumur, hundreds of miles from the fighting. In any case, as everyone knew, and even Churchill supposed, had not France the most powerful army in Europe? That was just one of many illusions that would be shattered so dramatically in the next four weeks when the tide of war moved on inexorably to the banks of the Loire and to Saumur, so long immured in its ancient traditions and its patriotic values and hence isolated from France's growing malaise now to be so tragically exposed.

2 Blitzkrieg

At first light on Friday 10 May 1940, Hitler dispatched his Panzers and his Stukas over the frontiers of the Netherlands, Belgium and Luxembourg in a devastatingly swift and powerful assault on Western Europe from the North Sea to the Moselle. In so doing, he shattered the unreality of the previous eight months. The Phoney War, the unofficial armed truce, was over, and although the German invasion of Denmark and Norway the previous month might well have served as a warning to the French High Command whose forces would have to bear the brunt of the fighting, those in authority, both in the Government and in the armed forces, reacted with a sluggish incomprehension or a misplaced confidence in military solutions, based on First World War experience, that were no longer relevant.

At the old fortress of Metz on the Moselle, General Georges Boris, Inspector General of Artillery, heard the sound of the guns and asked his aide, 'Where are they holding the manœuvres?'

'That, *mon général*,' said his aide, 'is the start of the German offensive.'

The Dutch and the Belgians, who had declared themselves neutral when the war started, seemed unwilling to accept that anything had changed. The mayor of Bouillon, an attractive little town in the Ardennes, had told General Huntziger's Second French Army that they could not requisition his hotels. 'Bouillon is a summer resort,' he said. 'Our hotels are reserved for tourists.' It seemed almost as if the Phoney War had been part of the German strategy, lulling the Allied armies on the Western Front into a feeling that there would not have to be any fighting anyway, that somehow a diplomatic solution to the current problems would be found.

A nineteenth-century Carrousel

The famous *Cadre Noir* of the Saumur Cavalry School 'are so skilled that they can do anything'

The Château of Saumur

It was difficult for the French to accept that it was all starting up again. They had lost 1½ million of their men during the First World War and seen the devastation of so many of their provinces in the north and east. The enthusiasm of August 1914, with its cries of '*à Berlin*' as France appeared to take its revenge for the defeat of 1870, did not exist in September 1939; there was only the resignation of '*Il faut en finir*' – 'It must be finished off.' Not a few remembered the prophetic words of Marshal Foch, who had led the Allied armies to victory in 1918: 'It is not a treaty of peace. It is a twenty-year armistice.' He had been referring in particular to the rejection of his plan for a permanent French occupation of the Rhineland in favour of a fifteen-year Allied occupation followed by demilitarization. Foch could, however, have been describing the general situation in Europe which after the 'twenty-year armistice' had brought a resumption of war.

France's concern between the two World Wars was to protect its frontiers against the invasion it had experienced in 1914; at vast expense the great Maginot Line of underground forts had been constructed along some 140 kilometres in the east to protect the important industrial provinces of Alsace and Lorraine, won back from Germany in 1918. Behind these fortifications the French felt secure. The events of May 1940, when the German armies demonstrated the irrelevance of the Maginot Line, were not only a shattering blow to French confidence, showing how misplaced this had been, but left the French High Command, whose thinking and planning were still on a First World War pattern, incapable of responding to the new situation.

General Gamelin, the French Commander-in-Chief, a close associate of Marshal Joffre in the First World War, was at his headquarters in the gloomy old fortress of Vincennes in Paris when the news of the German invasion of the Low Countries came in. He then did what the Germans hoped he would do. He ordered his best troops to take up positions deep inside Belgium. These included General Blanchard's First Army with its famous Cavalry Corps, the pride of Saumur, under General Prioux. It also included Lord Gort's ten divisions of the British Expeditionary Force. Eventually fifty-three Allied divisions took up the positions worked out for them by General Gamelin to meet the case of a German invasion of Belgium, where they would operate with the Belgian Army under the personal command of King Leopold II.

At Vincennes all was confidence. Gamelin was reported to be in good form, walking about, humming cheerfully and with 'a pleased and martial air'. In London *The Times* declared: 'This time at least there has been no strategic surprise', and its American colleague *The New York Times* was equally sanguine. None, however, was more pleased than the Germans themselves, since they were coming for the French by quite a different route, a route which the French had believed to be militarily impossible, the forest of the Ardennes, and in so doing they would come round the end of the Maginot Line. Gamelin's advance into Belgium was to prove even more dangerous to Allied prospects than his confidence in the Maginot Line, since it concentrated the attention of the Allies in the wrong place and cornered the most mobile part of their forces in the battle that developed there; these could not be extricated to deal with the main German threat coming through the Ardennes towards the Meuse river.

Back in 1934, Marshal Pétain had told the Army Commission of the French Senate that this Meuse sector was not in danger because the forest was impenetrable. General von Rundstedt's Army Group was quickly to show how wrong he had been. The French refused at first to believe that the German Panzers were moving through the trees. And, when the tanks emerged from the trees and started for the river, they came out just where Gamelin had his poorest troops, mostly reservists of the Second and Ninth Armies. Both French armies gave way before the power of the German thrust directed by the crack Panzer leader, General Guderian, whose men had rehearsed their forest manœuvres diligently. Before long they were on French territory.

After a day of merciless bombing by the Luftwaffe, Sedan, on the banks of the Meuse, surrendered late on 13 May. At Gamelin's headquarters at Vincennes, a staff officer later recalled, some of his fellow officers were '... quite openly sobbing at having to admit the shame they felt'. In the history of Franco-German conflict, Sedan was a symbol of psychological importance almost outweighing its military significance: here in

1870 the Emperor Napoleon III with 100,000 men had surrendered and been made prisoner. It was a humiliation that had been felt ever since, and not even the prolonged and determined defence of nearby Verdun in 1916 had obliterated it. Now it was all happening again.

There were disturbing reports of French troops cracking under strain and running away. General Giraud, who replaced General Corap in command of the Ninth Army, was soon to request that he be sent men who would not run away but would have themselves killed on the spot. During these days on the Meuse, as the Germans came out of the forest and advanced on the river, there were the first signs of the panic, of the disorder and indiscipline that in due course were to affect the whole country.

There was worse to come. The decisive date was 15 May, the date on which the battle for France in 1940 was really lost, for on that day the German Panzers broke out of the Meuse and it became clear that they could get behind the Allied armies that Gamelin had sent into Belgium and, by driving towards the Channel ports, could cut them off from the south. However, in Paris the Government, presided over by Paul Reynaud, and at Vincennes the military command continued to see everything as a repetition of the events of the First World War. In 1914 the Germans had been stopped by Marshal Joffre on the Marne just before Paris; now, it seemed, they were coming again.

In London, late on the afternoon of 14 May, Winston Churchill, who had become Britain's Prime Minister on the very day the Germans launched their attack on the West, received a telephone call from Reynaud asking for more British air squadrons. 'Germany is trying to deal us a fatal blow in the direction of Paris,' he said. At 7.30 the next morning Churchill was awakened by the telephone. It was Reynaud once more. 'We are beaten,' the French Prime Minister was saying. 'We have lost the battle. All is changed. A torrent of tanks is pouring through.' Churchill then telephoned General Georges, the French commander in the field, and received a less excited report. And from General Gamelin at Vincennes came a telegram in which the Commander-in-Chief said he viewed the situation with calm. But then Gamelin's imperturbability was such that he sometimes appeared to be out of touch with life itself.

On 16 May Churchill decided to fly to Paris with his advisers to find out for himself what was going on. It was the first of several journeys he was to make to France before the final drama on the banks of the Loire a month later. On that same afternoon that the cadets at Saumur were watching the arrival at their school of the horses and carriages of the King of the Belgians, in Paris British and French leaders were discussing the serious situation that had arisen. As they did so, Churchill could not but notice that in the grounds of the Quai d'Orsay, the French Foreign Ministry, they were already burning documents that ought not to fall into enemy hands if Paris were to be taken. It looked ominous. Nor was Churchill reassured when, asking Gamelin about French reserves, he was told frankly by the Commander-in-Chief that there were none. On that day Britain, with whom France had made a solemn agreement on 28 March that neither country would surrender without the permission of the other, was aware for the first time that France might be defeated. Certainly the French, at least those in authority, were pessimistic and defeatist, although at this stage, thanks to censorship and a general lack of information, the nation as a whole was still unaware of the disaster that was developing in the north.

That disaster had struck in an unexpected quarter just four days after the German assault had begun. The French had been shocked to discover that the forest of the Ardennes was not, as they had believed, impenetrable, and now the Germans had broken through their lines on the Meuse along an eighty-kilometre front from Dinant to Sedan, whose historic fortress had once more been surrendered humiliatingly to the enemy. On 13 and 14 May the Germans had secured bridgeheads over the river and on the fateful 15th seven Panzer divisions had broken out to head for the coast or for Paris or wherever they wished to go. The Panzer commander, General Guderian, was now putting a new idea into practice, with devastating effect: a long-range advance by tanks that could cut the arteries of an opposing army far back behind the front. The ill-fated General Huntziger, an aggressive and outstanding commander but with wretchedly inferior troops, had taken a severe mauling, while General Corap's Ninth Army had got into such disorder that the resourceful General Giraud had had to be sent from the Seventh Army to take charge of it. (This was the same General Giraud, who, later escaping from a German prison, would be picked up off the French Mediterranean coast by a British submarine and taken to North Africa, where he would become for a while the rival of General de Gaulle for the Free French leadership.)

Having battered the French Second and Ninth Armies on the Meuse, the Germans were now well on their way to achieving their aims, cutting off the Allied armies in Belgium up in the north. Gamelin now realized that the Germans had concentrated their main strength on the Meuse but he still gave no orders for the armies in Belgium to pull back; nor was any counter-offensive in the south forthcoming. However, by 18 May, as he was to state later in his memoirs, he knew that the Germans were not, after all, coming for Paris as they had in 1914, but were going for the Channel ports and would strike up from the rear of the French and British divisions in Belgium, seeking to encircle and destroy there the main Allied strength; after that they could turn south for the second phase of their campaign for the defeat of France.

None of this, however, was to be General Gamelin's concern any longer. Even before the start of the German offensive his Prime Minister, Reynaud, had wanted to get rid of him. Gamelin had been the choice of the previous premier, Daladier, who in the Reynaud Cabinet had become War Minister and then Foreign Minister, and at Daladier's insistence Gamelin had stayed on. This time, however, he had to go. Amiable, incredibly detached, Gamelin went home to his little flat in the Avenue Foch and, as André Maurois recorded, got out his typewriter and, seemingly oblivious of the approach of the war and the Germans, began to tap away at his memoirs, at sixty-seven already an old man, not really in touch with 1940, in spirit still back in 1914 with his old chief, General Joffre.

Reynaud's way of dealing with the crisis that was developing was even more surprising. Having got rid of Joffre's man from World War I, he summoned back to France from Beirut Marshal Foch's old chief-of-staff, General Weygand, aged seventy-four. Weygand had retired from the Army in 1935 and had been out of touch with it until the outbreak of war, when he had come back to take command in the Lebanon of France's forces in the Middle East. He received Reynaud's summons on 16 May and two days later landed – in fact, ominously crash-landed – outside Paris, to find that in the midst of the growing débâcle, he was expected to devise a plan to save France. At the same time Reynaud called back to France his Ambassador in Spain, another father-figure from the First World War, the eighty-four-year-old Marshal Pétain, to join the Cabinet as its vice-president.

France could hardly be saved by its ancient monuments but Reynaud no doubt thought that the presence of Pétain and Weygand would help restore the morale of Frenchmen and in particular of French soldiers. As Reynaud was soon to find to his cost, however, all he had done was to strengthen the pessimistic and defeatist elements in his hierarchy and give them a centre to focus on. He had actually chosen two distinguished figures from the past who believed that the rottenness of the present, the social and moral decay in France, had been caused by its politicians and ought not to be preserved at the cost of the lives of French soldiers. This was a view that grew stronger as the military situation deteriorated. General Sikorski, commanding Polish forces in France, was disturbed to hear Weygand say that France had to endure suffering as punishment for its twenty years of laxity. To Sikorski, Weygand seemed to be confusing his roles. 'As a Catholic you may talk like this, but not as Commander-in-Chief,' he said.

In the next few weeks Weygand, the cavalryman, pupil and Chief Instructor at Saumur, deeply steeped in the values of its Cavalry School, professional soldier *par excellence*, would reiterate again and again the overriding importance of upholding the honour of the Army. At one stage it seemed to General Spears, Churchill's personal representative with Reynaud, that Weygand was even drawing a distinction between the honour of the Army and the honour of France, implying that the first could not be sacrificed to the second. But, then, in Weygand's eyes, the Army *was* the nation, and hence their honour was indivisible.

Returned to France and given greater power as Supreme Commander than Gamelin had enjoyed, Weygand applied himself with energy and enthusiasm to tackling the tremendous task he had accepted. He quit the dismal Château de Vincennes, described by de Gaulle as 'a submarine without a periscope', where Gamelin had directed his efforts, and took up quarters at Montry, outside Paris. One of his officers, Captain André Beaufre, recorded that Weygand had taken up '… the burden of command with a daring, a passion, and a fierce will which was a total contrast to the pale, stiff calm of his predecessor … elegant, neat and poised, direct, kind but often curt and easily moved to terseness, he gave the impression of intense personal energy, coupled with an astonishing physical stamina'. He was constantly on the move, visiting his troops, flying to the cut-off armies in Belgium, conferring with the King of the Belgians; despite his age, a spry little figure, fit and tough, demonstrating at one point to his officers that he could sprint 100 metres and take stairs four at a time on his way to the conference room.

However, the disaster that was beginning to loom over France's armed forces, and over the country as a whole, would prove too much for Weygand, who, as setback followed setback, increasingly took on the role of Cassandra, ably supported at every turn by Marshal Pétain, who while still in Madrid had been heard to say the previous March, 'France's greatest mistake has been to enter this war', a remark which, reported to Germany, gave comfort to those directing the war from Berlin.

'Brisk, buoyant and incisive' was how Churchill described Weygand when, back in Paris with his advisers, he heard from the new French C-in-C how he was going to tackle the German threat. Weygand's plan envisaged aggressive action against the German incursion, with the armies in the north attacking southward and those in the south moving northward. The plan looked sound enough but had not taken account of the fact that the Allied forces in Belgium had already taken tremendous punishment. The German drive to the Channel ports kept on, and the British Expeditionary Force, fearing encirclement, was now withdrawing as rapidly as possible for Dunkirk and evacuation. Weygand's plan never got underway and as time went on he was to reserve for the British a good portion of the blame.

By the last days of May the Germans had successfully sealed off the great Allied army that Gamelin had dispatched northwards with such confidence only three weeks earlier. Evacuation by sea from Dunkirk was the only solution – but would it be possible? The capitulation of the Belgian Army under King Leopold on 28 May made evacuation even more hazardous. Then came an inexplicable action by Hitler: he stopped the advance of the German armour; the foremost tanks were ordered to hold their positions until the troops in the rear had closed up. But for the German tanks on this sector it was the end of the road; they were transferred to the German armies in the east, where they were soon to be employed in the second part of the German offensive, the attack across the Somme and the Aisne into the heart of France. The Luftwaffe was given the task of dealing with the British and French forces waiting inside the small perimeter round Dunkirk to be lifted to safety by the Royal Navy and the French fleet.

However, despite everything the Luftwaffe attempted, it could not stop the Royal Navy's 'Operation Dynamo', which, beginning on Sunday 26 May, eventually brought back to Britain not only a quarter of a million members of the British Expeditionary Force but 115,000 French soldiers, too.

The part played at Dunkirk by the former Commandant of the Cavalry School of Saumur, General de la Laurencie, was to receive special praise in British accounts of the evacuation, notably in the diary of Sir Alexander Cadogan, head of the Foreign Office. Determined that his Third Corps, should escape captivity, de la Laurencie urged his exhausted troops to make a sixty-kilometre night march along the crowded roads through Poperinge and Hondschoote to reach Dunkirk in the early hours of 29 May. Although compelled to leave most of their equipment at Dunkirk, they were lifted safely to Britain, and in due course General de la Laurencie, like his fellow cavalryman Colonel du Vigier of the 3rd Light Mechanized Division (DLM) got back to France, reformed his men and took part in the final phase along the Loire in the battle for France.

For the British, whose army had been saved and, re-equipped, would live to fight another day, Dunkirk was an occasion for thanksgiving. Its significance in British military history is different from that placed on it in French accounts of these unhappy days. For the French, Dunkirk brought to an end the first phase in the defeat of France in 1940. The northern armies had been lost and, although thousands of French soldiers had been lifted to safety in Britain, and would find their way back to France, they had lost their equipment and were merely the remnants of what had been whole units.

At the end of May Weygand was considering how to deal with the much more serious situation that had developed. He became increasingly gloomy. Back in the military headquarters of Vincennes, whose atmosphere reflected his mood, he had a meeting with Baudouin, one of Reynaud's ministers, who left an account of the interview in which the French Commander-in-Chief spoke of how he saw the situation developing after the loss of the armies in the north. He could now call on only fifty divisions, and these would have to hold a front of 180 miles from the Somme and the Aisne as far as the Maginot Line. 'Fifty divisions along this front would only constitute a sand dune,' he was saying, 'and would not be able to withstand the pressure of fifteen divisions and ten armoured divisions.... I think that, if there is a surrender in the north, the French Army ought to resist desperately on the Somme and Aisne positions. Then, when the enemy has broken this resistance, what is left of the French Army should continue to fight where it stands until it is annihilated.' According to Baudouin, Weygand, having discussed with him the state of France, confessed, '... with tears in his eyes', that he doubted if the country's morale would support a fight to the bitter end.

If, as Weygand decided, the army was to fight on for the sake of honour, despite the unequal contest in numbers and equipment, then all the rivers of France, not just the Somme and the Aisne, where the second phase of the German offensive would begin, would have to be defended. Consequently at the end of May Weygand put out an instruction to all the commanders of the military regions of France 'to bring to a state of defence all the rivers that could bar the invasion route to the south'.

Among those who received this order was General Vary, commanding the 9th Military Region at Tours, the main town on the Loire, who immediately called a meeting of his senior officers in the area. To his assistant, General Pichon, he delegated the duty of allotting to these various commanders a particular sector of the river to defend. Pichon, anticipating the future, had already been doing his homework. As early as 18 May, as General Weygand was arriving back in France from the Middle East, he had had a meeting at Orléans, up river from Tours, with the general commanding the 5th Military Region, and together they had worked out plans for the defence of the Loire and the exploitation of whatever armaments they could get hold of. By the end of May, when Weygand's instruction was received, Pichon already knew what he had to do. However, what he and his fellow commanders had in mind were plans to cope with marauding advance elements of the German Army, reconnaissance or raiding parties. No one could have imagined that what they would in fact have to deal with was the full might of the German Panzers.

It was at this stage, at the end of May, that General Pichon came to see the Commandant of the Cavalry School, who learned that he might be given the responsibility of defending the river along a forty-kilometre front that stretched from Gennes, west of Saumur, to Montsoreau, east of the town. General Pichon knew the Cavalry School and its Commandant, Colonel Michon very well; his own son Louis had passed out top of the previous year's course, and he was confident that the school, aided by the diverse elements that he would eventually assign to Colonel Michon's command, would do its duty.

However, in his enthusiasm to organize the defence of the Loire from local military resources, General Pichon was calling upon some who were under the direct authority of the War Ministry and not of any general in the field. The Cavalry School, being an educational establishment and not a military unit, was the responsibility of the Director of Cavalry at the War Ministry and not of the High Command conducting military operations. In due course, this was to cause confusion both to General Pichon and to the Commandant of the School, Colonel Michon, though, in the general confusion that had overtaken the country as a whole by the time fighting started on the Loire, this was a minor consideration and in the end, despite conflicting orders, the Commandant, his teaching staff of instructors and their cadets would do what they had already resolved to do.

With Dunkirk now over, General Weygand determined to make one last supreme effort on the Somme and along the Aisne to stop the German advance. If he could have done this by rhetoric alone, victory would certainly have been his. He had told Baudouin on 24 May: 'The army must resist firmly in the Somme-Aisne position and when this resistance is broken, the fragments must stand fast to the end to save our honour.' At a meeting of the War Council the following day, he repeated his intention of making one great effort on the Somme-Aisne line: 'The present position must be maintained. It may crumble … the fragments will form breakwaters. Each part of the army must fight to the end in defence of honour.' Long after, Weygand recalled: 'I had had this solution in mind from the first; defence to the death in the Somme-Aisne position.' On 26 May he issued a General Order containing the following stirring message: 'The battle on which the fate of the country depends will be fought on our present position, without thought of withdrawal. All leaders, down to the platoon commanders, must be imbued with a fierce desire to fight to the death.'

Weygand was offering his army heroic words but it was like whistling in the wind. He had his doubts about whether the troops would fight to the death. On the day he issued his General Order he told Baudouin: 'If we succumb, I shall have the ghastly job of meeting the Germans, just as at Réthondes twenty-two years ago but with the positions reversed.' Having accompanied Marshal Foch to the railway carriage at Compiègne in 1918 and as his chief-of-staff read out the armistic terms to the defeated Germans, he seems in May-June 1940 to have been haunted by the prospect of having to return there, and in due course he would categorically refuse to do so.

On 29 May, while the Dunkirk evacuation was going on, Weygand told the Government that, 'A moment may well come when France, however unwilling, may find it impossible to continue military operations in defence of her homeland.' This thought of defeat had been at the back of the minds of Government ministers and the High Command since the German break-out on the Meuse on 15 May, in fact before Weygand's return to France – 'a doctor called in at the last moment to heal a man dying of an incurable disease', as one of his staff officers, Captain André Beaufre, was to write. 'We felt ourselves beaten,' said Beaufre, 'but no one would admit it until our defeat was absolute. It seemed that thus the honour of our army would be saved.'

Weygand's fine rhetoric on the eve of the Somme battle seemed to be out of keeping with reality, even with his own innermost thoughts at the time, and yet when the battle began, on 5 June, it seemed at first that the words of the

Commander-in-Chief had gone home. The German commander, General List, reported: 'No signs of demoralization are evident anywhere. We are seeing a new French way of fighting.' These were the soldiers to whom Weygand had said: 'May the thought of our afflicted country inspire in you an unflinching resolve to stand firm. The fate of our country and the future of our children depend on your firmness.'

On Weygand's orders his troops were fighting from a checkerwork of closed operational bases called hedgehogs, installed in the villages and woods and packed with 75mm guns mounted as anti-tank weapons. 'This', said General Réquin, commanding Fourth Army, 'was only a last resort to enable these weak but brave troops to resist with honour before being overwhelmed.' And so it was. It only temporarily halted the Germans. Rommel's Panzers found a way round the hedgehogs, and once again the French were shown to be fighting the war of 1940 with the static defences of the 1914-18 combats. Only de Gaulle, who had led a successful attack around Laon with tanks and who had now become a junior minister in the Reynaud Government, was calling for the army to keep on the move – to manœuvre, manœuvre. It was – but once again in retreat, towards the Seine and towards Paris.

To Weygand the situation appeared increasingly to be without hope. At a conference on 9 June he said: 'Our armies are fighting the last possible defensive battle. If this attempt fails, they are doomed to destruction.' The next day he sent a note to the Prime Minister, saying, 'The ultimate failure of our lines may occur at any moment ... our armies would then fight to the end but their collapse would only be a question of time.' That same day, 10 June, the Germans crossed the Seine, and the Government decided to quit Paris for Tours, thus repeating the pattern of 1870 in that other war against Germany. Weygand, too, withdrew his headquarters to the Loire, to Briare. Then the news came through that Italy had entered the war on Hitler's side.

On 8 June de Gaulle, in his capacity as Under-Secretary of State for War, had called on Weygand at his Montry headquarters and found him 'calm and master of himself'. The C-in-C told de Gaulle: 'You see, I was not mistaken when I told you a few days ago that the Germans would attack on the

Somme on 6 June. They are in fact attacking. At this moment they are crossing the river. I can't stop them.'

'All right', said de Gaulle. 'They're crossing the Somme. And then?'

'Then,' said Weygand, 'the Seine and the Marne.'

'And then?' de Gaulle persisted.

'And then? Then? But that's the end,' said Weygand.

'How do you mean, the end?' asked de Gaulle. 'What about the world, and the empire?'

'That's childish', said Weygand. 'As for the world, when I've been beaten here, England won't wait a week before negotiating with the Reich.'

De Gaulle left it at that and returned to Paris.

At Briare Weygand took stock of the position and decided on a general retreat southwards of all his forces. In the next few days a kind of dreadful inevitability seemed to take over in France, as in a Greek tragedy. Weygand seemed to lose interest in the military operations and concentrated his efforts on persuading the Government to seek an armistice. He wrote long afterwards: 'I had provided the best conditions for the retreat but at this juncture my role at GHQ was to take a back seat. My duties of advising the Government were becoming all-important and would take up most of my time.'

On 11 June Winston Churchill with his senior advisers flew to Briare to consult with the French on the critical situation that now faced them. His concern was how to keep France in the war now that its armies were overwhelmed, how to prevent France from making a separate peace with Germany. The French Government was clearly split – ironically it was the two famous soldiers, Pétain and Weygand, who were leading the faction that was pressing for an armistice. The Prime Minister, Reynaud, and his supporters, including de Gaulle, wanted the Government to move to North Africa and, with the French empire and fleet intact, to continue the war alongside Britain. There was even talk of turning Brittany into a fortress where the remnants of the French Army might re-group. Little by little, however, the persistent pessimism of Pétain and Weygand gained ground. Weygand was contemptuous of any future effort by Britain to continue the fight although after Dunkirk Britain had sent back to France a force under General Sir Alan Brooke, known as Normanforce, to continue resistance in France. Britain would have its neck wrung like a chicken, he said – a remark that provoked Churchill's famous rejoinder, 'Some chicken! Some neck!'

Two days later Churchill was once more back on the Loire, this time at Tours* for a meeting with the War Council. By now Paris was in German hands, French resistance on the Seine and Marne had crumbled, and Weygand had ordered the general retreat. If the French were to offer any further resistance, it would have to be on the banks of the Loire itself. But the French crisis had now split its Cabinet; there seemed little more that Britain could do, and Lord Beaverbrook, who was with Churchill, said, 'Let's go home.'

A further meeting with the French Government had been due to take place at the Château de Cangé, where President Lebrun had established temporary quarters, but this was now cancelled. Nevertheless, members of the War Council turned up, and they were annoyed to find that Churchill was not, after all, going to be present. The meeting produced acrimonious exchanges between Reynaud and Weygand. The General's almost mystical views about the Army and its honour came more and more to the fore in argument. Weygand had a soldier's dislike of politicians and, as he saw it, they – Reynaud in particular – were prepared to sacrifice the honour of the Army in the interest of the Government's continuing the war from North Africa. What Reynaud wanted his Commander-in-Chief to do was to follow the example of the Dutch and the Belgians, for the Army to capitulate while the Government carried on the war from elsewhere. The Army would surrender but not the country or the nation. Such a suggestion drove Weygand, the professional soldier, into a hysterical fury. According to Yves Bouthillier, one of the French ministers present, Weygand's reply to Reynaud's suggestion of a capitulation was, 'I would never agree to bring such disgrace on the flags of the French Army.'

Later there was a further exchange between the Prime Minister and his Commander-in-Chief.

* Visitors to the Prefecture at Tours are today shown with pride a burn mark on a desk which was made, they are told, by Churchill's cigar.

Reynaud: 'You are going to have to make the Army capitulate, General.'

Weygand: 'There is no power in the world that would make me sign the capitulation of an army that has just fought as the French Army has.'

Reynaud: 'You will do it if I give you the order.'

Weygand: 'Never! You won't find one French soldier who would accept such a humiliation.'

Reynaud: 'You are here to obey.'

Weygand: 'I'm here to defend the honour of the Army. You and the President are trying to evade your responsibility. The Government took the responsibility of declaring war – it must shoulder the responsibility for the armistice.'

General Weygand never changed this view. In due course he wrote: 'I rejected the proposal with indignation. I will never agree to inflict such shame on our flag. This would have been the ultimate crime, damning and doing irreparable harm to the military honour of our nation, a crime which the Military Code of Justice punishes with death.... I cannot think of such an ignominious proposal without a shiver of disgust.'

In 1940 Weygand, the product of Saumur with its ancient concepts of military honour, was faced with an intolerable dilemma that made of him (in the words of F.C.P. Bankwitz, one of his biographers) an 'authentically tragic figure in modern French history', a military commander whose total devotion to the Army deprived him of 'an accurate view of the world and the true significance of his acts'. In his stance he appeared to be illogical and contradictory. Since the French Army in his eyes had no option but to continue to fight until it was annihilated (for that was what honour demanded), the State, France itself, must secure an armistice from the enemy in order to prevent such a sacrifice. As General Spears noted at the time and others have noted since, Weygand apparently considered it less dishonourable for France to give up the common fight of its entire sea, air and overseas land forces still in combat than to surrender merely the Army on metropolitan soil – which was in fact soil no longer under French control.

On the evening of 12 June, after ordering the general retreat of French forces and calling on the Government to seek an armistice, he made his view clearer as to the honour of the Army. 'The main thing is to avoid a total disintegration of the Army and so we should ask the German Government for an armistice forthwith. France can now request an armistice without blushing. I am proud to have fought on the Somme a battle restoring the true honour of the French Army. It has defended honour and henceforward negotiation will no longer be unworthy of it.'

Again at the meeting at Cangé at which Churchill had been expected to be present, he said: 'If we wish to save the discipline of the Army, we must rapidly obtain a cessation of hostilities.'

At this point Marshal Pétain added his voice: 'The armistice is inevitable. It should be requested without delay.'

Twenty-five years later Reynaud and Weygand were still arguing the merits of their respective views of June 1940. In an open letter to the *Figaro* newspaper, Weygand, by then in his mid-nineties, told the former premier: 'I am a man of honour and a man of order. Order is the health of the State.' Weygand was objecting to Reynaud's claim that the General, in his views about order, had been encroaching on the political field in June 1940 when he had envisaged keeping the Army intact in order to preserve the civil order in France, something that would be impossible once the Army, without an armistice, had been destroyed by the enemy. Hence there had to be an armistice.*

As Reynaud, Mandel, the Interior Minister, and others who favoured continuing the war from outside France went on resisting Weygand and Pétain's plea for an armistice, the Commander-in-Chief began to react ever more vociferously against the civil power in France. He even accused the Government of cowardice in having abandoned Paris: they should have awaited the Germans there as the Roman senators had waited for the Barbarians. He then interpreted the Government's plan to withdraw from France to North Africa in

* In 1980 to mark the fortieth anniversary of the armistice, *Le Figaro* conducted a poll among 1,000 people to obtain their views on what had happened. A big majority believed that Pétain had acted with the best motives and that the armistice had been a good thing for France and the French. Signing the armistice was approved by fifty-three per cent with only twenty-six per cent believing that the Government ought to have gone to North Africa.

)n 17 June 1940 Marshal Pétain roadcasts: 'The fighting must ease'. The cadets wept with rage

On 18 June 1940 General de Gaulle broadcasts from London: 'Soldiers of France, wherever you are, arise!' The cadets were the first *résistants*

21 June 1940 – Armistice in the railway carriage at Compiègne. While General Huntziger faces Hitler, the cadets at Saumur resist heroically

April 1940 – the cadets assemble for their course

Lieutenant-Colonel Trambly de Laissardière (*centre*) competing at Wembley in 1934 when he won the Prince of Wales Cup. In June 1940 at Saumur he saved the horses

the same way. It would be cowardly to leave, he maintained. The Government ought to have the courage to stay in France, if only because the French people would not otherwise accept the sacrifice that would be demanded of them. The Government would lose its authority over them if it departed. He himself would never leave France under any conditions, not even if he were put in irons. Having made his point melodramatically, he stormed out of the meeting of ministers at Cangé.

The campaign Weygand was now waging was one of intimidation, not only to bring about the cessation of hostilities in France but against the removal of the Government to the North African empire. His fellow campaigner, the most prestigious member of the Reynaud Cabinet, was a Marshal of France, Philippe Pétain. As German propaganda posters showing his photograph were soon to ask – 'Can you be more French than he?' However, Reynaud, too, was speaking of honour, the honour of France itself, not just the honour of the Army. Here were two different conceptions of honour, two different conceptions of priorities, the nation or its army. It was not a new argument in France; forty years earlier it had revolved around the Dreyfus case.

At the château of Cangé on the Loire on 13 June 1940 Reynaud put as strongly as he could the case for the honour of France: whatever France now decided to do, the war would go on; the blockade of France by Britain and the occupation of France by Germany were inevitable. The French people would be prisoners, and if France now broke its solemn agreement with Britain not to make a separate peace with Germany, it would be left without hope. 'To ask for an armistice with Germany would therefore be to lose both honour and hope,' he maintained.

Inside the Cabinet the factions pulled this way and that, but little by little the convictions of the Commander-in-Chief began to gain weight as military reality in the shape of the German advance south came closer. The Panzers were now moving on the Loire itself, both in the west and in the east. It was no longer safe for the Government to stay at Tours, and on 14 June it began to withdraw to Bordeaux, as had another French Government in the conflict with Germany in 1870. Weygand and his staff quit Briare for Vichy, having first discussed with

General Alan Brooke the continuation of Anglo-French military co-operation in Brittany. The British field commander, however, was convinced that the military position was lost, that the idea of creating a Breton Redoubt was not feasible. Soon after this the British troops were detached from Weygand's command, and their evacuation from France was ordered.

The French Cabinet continued to seesaw. Reynaud realized he would have to get rid of Weygand, who appeared to be occupying himself increasingly with political policy. The Prime Minister had been surprised to discover that Weygand, through his military attaché in London, had been responsible for bringing Churchill to his headquarters at Briare on 11 June. De Gaulle had earlier discussed with Reynaud the need to remove Weygand and, with Reynaud's permission, had approached General Huntziger, who, according to de Gaulle, had agreed to take over if he were asked. But it was already too late. Events were moving too fast.

Losing support in his own Cabinet, Reynaud appealed to President Roosevelt for America to come to France's aid, but Roosevelt was unable to give him the support he wanted since this would have meant a declaration of war by the United States against Germany. Then Reynaud agreed to a clever suggestion by one of his ministers, Chautemps, that Germany should be asked what the conditions of an armistice would be if France were to ask for one, Chautemps insisting not very convincingly that to ask for the conditions of an armistice was not the same as asking for an armistice. This could be made acceptable to the British Government, it was argued. Churchill agreed on the understanding that the question of the future of the French fleet should remain outside any kind of armistice discussion.

Finally, as the French ship of state began to sink and with it Reynaud and his faction, on 16 June in a bold and imaginative stroke Winston Churchill offered a union of Britain and France as a single state – but the offer drew only contempt from Pétain and others of his faction. It was nevertheless an historic event: not since the days of the Plantagenets, whose tombs appropriately were on the Loire, had France and England been part of one another.* De Gaulle telephoned Reynaud from

* British Cabinet papers researched by Dr John Zametica and referred to by

London, giving the text of what the British Cabinet had agreed – that Britain and France should be no longer two nations but form one indissoluble union, that France was to keep its available forces in the field, on the sea and in the air and that the Union was to concentrate its whole energy against the power of the enemy. It had come too late. Before the arrival of the offer Pétain had announced his resignation from the Government but Reynaud had persuaded him to stay until they had heard from President Roosevelt. When Roosevelt, as explained earlier, had to disappoint Reynaud, he played his final card – the union with Britain. As President Lebrun was to write later: 'The Council was greatly surprised at this ... in such an unfavourable atmosphere this project only met with a tepid welcome, despite the support of the President of the Council [Reynaud] and myself.'

Debate in the Government became increasingly acrimonious, with references to *capitulards* and *déserteurs*, to cowardice on one side or the other. The Cabinet was in a state of decomposition. Reynaud was not obliged to resign. He could have formed another Cabinet or he could have sacked his Commander-in-Chief, Weygand, but there was an atmosphere of alarm and urgency which made such actions unlikely.

While the Cabinet was meeting at Cangé, President Lebrun read the latest alarming dispatches from General Georges on the military situation: the Germans were at Dijon and on the Saône and their armoured columns were approaching La Charité-sur-Loire. Urgent political decisions were necessary in the interests of the military.

Reynaud had come to the end. The normally dynamic little man was exhausted and could no longer resist the entreaties of his mistress, the Comtesse de Portes, to give up. Realizing that he no longer commanded a majority in face of the Chautemps demand that France should ask Germany for the conditions of an armistice, he resigned, telling President Lebrun he would

---

The Sunday Times on 6 September 1987 reveal surprisingly that on 11 September 1956, shortly before the outbreak of the Suez crisis involving France and Britain, the French Prime Minister, Guy Mollet, asked the British Premier, Anthony Eden, if it might be possible to resurrect the 1940 idea of an Anglo-French union.

have to find a new leader for the Government.

'But who?' asked Lebrun.

'You'll have no difficulty,' replied Reynaud. 'The Marshal told me this morning that he had his Cabinet in his pocket.'

'I summoned the Marshal then,' recorded Lebrun. 'I asked him to form a Cabinet. A pleasant surprise for me.' Pétain opened his briefcase and presented the president with the list of his ministers.

Shortly after midnight the new Foreign Minister, Baudouin, through the Spanish Ambassador, set in train France's request to Germany for the conditions of an armistice. The following day General Spears, Churchill's representative with Reynaud, flew back to London, and in due course the Royal Navy sent a destroyer to pick up the British Ambassador, Sir Ronald Campbell.

In the week that had gone since the Germans had marched down the Champs Elysées, and while French ministers, first at Tours, then at Bordeaux, had been arguing among themselves, revealing a squalid clash of personalities and a seeking after power (some were already looking ahead beyond the demise of the Third Republic to a new authoritarian order) – while all this was going on, France itself was becoming increasingly chaotic. Panic and pandemonium were taking over as communication broke down and, in the absence of information, rumour abounded. Without effective leadership from the Government and as direction from the High Command grew ever more uncertain, France's disintegrating armies were having to fend for themselves. One thought seemed to be uppermost – keep moving south to escape capture by the ever-advancing Germans.

In the new Pétain Government, General Weygand had become Minister of National Defence, so he was now both politician and soldier. The politician had sought and was now awaiting the outcome of the armistice request but the soldier was insisting that the Army must still resist and that it should not stop fighting until the Government ordered it to do so. This situation became increasingly confused. The following day, 17 June, Marshal Pétain as France's new Prime Minister broadcast his message to the nation, saying, 'We must stop the fighting.' Many units interpreted this as calling for them to lay down their arms, and many did so, but the Commander-in-Chief General Weygand was insisting that fighting must not stop, that while the armistice was unsigned it was the duty of French soldiers to resist the enemy.

The Marshal's words had had a devastating effect on the Cavalry cadets at Saumur. Since France was in touch with the enemy about an armistice, the war was already lost. A battle fought now could have only one purpose – to allow a soldier to save his honour. For most of France, civilians and soldiers, to ask for an armistice and to go on fighting made no sense, and so, while the cadets of Saumur were obeying atavistic voices from the past, they also had to listen to jeers and insults from the contemporary world, from those who, like spectators at a football match, were running over the field where players were waiting to meet their adversary, and in so doing confused further, both physically and morally, the young pupil soldiers who had not yet seen a battle fought. Their field of battle had been invaded by the refugees, whose sole concern was to get safely across the Loire and who now jammed the approach roads to the bridges. If the scenes were appalling, they were also sometimes incongruous: at one place a general, wearing his gold-leafed kepi, was diverting traffic from his troops as if he were a common *gendarme* on point duty.

The flight of the civilians towards the south had begun at the start of the German onslaught on the Low Countries nearly six weeks earlier, a small stream at first of Dutch and Belgians, who, trying to escape from the war, had been crossing France's northern frontier. For a while the French had tried to stop them there but later, as their numbers increased dramatically, there was neither the will nor the means to stop them. The more the people took to the roads, the more panic and rumour took over. Captain André Maurois described what he saw in Belgium: 'The whole village, infected with a collective panic would leave with its mayor, its *curé*, its town officers. The roads were flooded with refugees. It was an amazing spectacle. First came the cars of the rich, driven by chauffeurs wearing gloves: then those of the middle classes, driven by their owners, with a mattress tied across the top; then the big country carts drawn by horses and carrying whole families, then platoons, battalions, armies of cyclists, to whom the red blanket tied to the bicycle frames gave a brilliant colour that would have delighted a painter; finally came a heart-rending procession of those on foot.'

What Maurois had seen early on in the German offensive was to grow in scale and intensity as that offensive not only overwhelmed the Low Countries but brought more and more of France's own territory under German control. 'At one point', Alistair Horne has written, 'it was estimated that as many as two million Dutch and Belgians and nearly eight million French refugees were on the roads, some nine-tenths of the population of a city like Lille departed. During the first five days of the battle the French kept the Belgian frontier closed. Then the human flood burst into northern France, resembling more one of the great migrations fleeing before the Barbarians in times of yore than any event hitherto seen in modern Europe.'

Weygand has used that expression, 'the Barbarians', when he blamed the Government for having quit Paris instead of waiting like the Roman senators for the Barbarians to arrive. But Paris, where at first so many of the refugees had been received with kindness and given shelter, then turned to blaming and cursing them in the general panic and disorder that overtook the French capital when, abandoned by the Government, it was declared an open city. Within a couple of days, in an atmosphere of *sauve qui peut* – each man for himself, a million Parisians had swelled the moving masses going south towards the Loire.

Hervé Alphand, who became France's Ambassador in Washington soon after the war, recorded in his journal on 11 June 1940: 'On the road from Chartres to Tours an immense convoy of refugees. The great wagons drawn by horses, carrying women in tears and children and with which are mixed lorries, touring cars, motorcycles in a frightful chaos. France is in flight and this enormous movement not only attacks the morale of a whole nation but impedes military operations that are still possible. The Government powerless can only let it go on and even seems to set an example. I look at these roads and fields with desolation as if I may never see them again.'

How had it all happened and who was responsible? Duff Cooper, one of Churchill's ministers in Paris ten days before Hervé Alphand's journey to Tours, recorded: 'I remember that on the following morning, one of the loveliest June days imaginable, Jean Giraudoux published an article in which he said that even to think that defeat was possible was an act of treason. Had that been true, there must have been many traitors in Paris that day.'

'*Nous sommes trahis*' – 'We have been betrayed': so often the cry of the French when overtaken by national disaster, and '*Je ne joue plus*' – 'I won't play any longer', when the game goes against them. Even the weather had betrayed them, it seemed in those fateful days of 1940, as day after day saw cloudless blue skies, endless sunshine enhancing the beauty of France and of its capital city as they were taken by the enemy, and on the crowded roads heat added to the fatigue of thirsty, hungry people who had fled their homes and did not know where they were going. Clear skies also made the task easier for the German aircraft which dived low over the defenceless refugees, firing into their midst and adding to their terror. The chaos created by the flight of millions of civilians mingled with the French soldiery made its contribution, too, and the Germans skilfully added to this chaos by infiltrating their own people among the fleeing civilians, passing them off as Belgians or Dutch. Two of these agents in disguise were to end their days in the combat at Saumur.

Although the role of the Fifth Column may have been exaggerated at the time, the fear and suspicion that German agents were able to spread among an already terrorized population on the run were real enough. As the poet Jean Cocteau was to say: 'All you see now on the roads of France are nuns winding on their puttees.' No priest was considered a priest any more; an officer in uniform might prove to be a false officer; authentic telephone messages were received with suspicion. Another poet, Paul Valéry, wrote: 'Nothing that we could fear is impossible; we can fear and imagine absolutely everything.'

Fear, disillusion, disgust, anger – all these emotions came to the surface in the critical last days of the battle of France when it reached the Loire in mid-June and set Frenchman against Frenchman, not only within the Government but through the nation as a whole and, perhaps, most particularly among the disintegrating armies, thousands of whose soldiers appeared to have lost or deserted their units and, haggard and dishevelled, were fleeing with the rest.

President Lebrun, who had been told by Commander-in-Chief Weygand that the armies had been defeated, was dismayed to find on his journey south from Tours to Bordeaux crowds of idle servicemen wandering around the towns and villages who had never been in action. General Spears, also on his way to Bordeaux, recorded that, 'Nearly all the towns and villages that I passed through were full of gaping, idle soldiers ... how came it that we were constantly told that all resources and manpower had been exhausted?'

It was not only military manpower that was neglected: the Germans were to find vast quantities of military supplies untouched in their depots, including tanks, anti-tank guns, shells by the million.

Weygand's aide, Captain Beaufre, going south to join his chief in the final days, wrote: 'During our short stops our role was now confined to discussions with the civil and military authorities as to whether there was still anywhere to fight or whether to press on down the road. Each seemed equally absurd. Here, at Vierzon, a tank officer who wanted to defend the outskirts of the town was killed by the population to save their homes from destruction; there, at Clermont-Ferrand, the troops were confined to barracks for an orderly surrender when the Germans arrived, while the General went off on his own. We tried to make the civil authorities, who too often were giving way to the general panic, stay at their posts.'

As military communication and command faltered, discipline collapsed. There were instances of insults to officers – at Nantes mud was thrown at an officer through the window of his car; on another occasion housewives seized the rifles of retreating soldiers so that resistance should cease. On all sides there was shame, humiliation and disgrace. And all the while the sun beat down through the long days from cloudless blue skies and at night exhausted, homeless Frenchmen lay down in ditches by the roadside in bright moonlight under the stars. Those who survived those days and nights described them as unreal, the grotesque juxtaposition of the ugliness of war with the beauty of France in midsummer's holiday weather.

So the war reached the Loire – and Saumur, where France is at its most romantically beautiful. 'A strange feeling came over me at this stage,' wrote André Beaufre twenty-five years later, by then one of his country's most distinguished generals. 'The war was now spreading into the land of my childhood. It seemed incredible to me that this peaceful valley of the Loire in which I had so often canoed and bathed, could become a theatre of war. I had never imagined that this could happen but here it was. When we pulled out of Briare in a long line of trucks and crossed the Loire, we saw bombers destroying Gien seven miles north of us. Along the road ahead of us an Italian fighter was shooting up the refugees.'

Further down the Loire, at Saumur, they were also attacking from the air. During the night of 8/9 June an air raid killed three people and caused damage near the railway station, and on the afternoon of 13 June there were further victims during an air raid on nearby Souzay. 'The Loire is going to become a major centre of operations,' Instructor Lieutenant de Galbert told his companions as they stood in the courtyard of the Cavalry School, still unaware of, or unwilling to know, the fate that was being decided for France by its political and military leaders only seventy kilometres upstream at Tours.

In that extraordinary June of 1940 there was even something unreal about the river itself, as if it too were playing the enemy's game. It had changed its usual habits. Normally in February the Loire would be in full flood at Saumur, its water swelling to the edges of its banks, but that year, at the end of winter, the river was low and remained so in the first days of spring. Then suddenly, at the beginning of May, it became a roaring torrent and continued so until the beginning of June, those who lived near its banks expecting it to flood over. No army, not even the Wehrmacht of 1940, advancing with all the confidence of victories already won, would have been able to cross without the greatest difficulty. Then suddenly again, in a matter of days, the waters were gone in front of Saumur, though they were still flowing fast under the bombed bridges at Gien, drowning some of the refugees fleeing from the war. At Saumur and along the forty-kilometre front that the Commandant of the Cavalry School was about to defend, the sandbanks appeared above the water and dried in the hot sun.

Colonel Michon, directing his military gaze from a position high up by the château of Saumur, from which he could see almost the whole of his sector of the Loire, observed grimly that they had already been betrayed by their own river.

3 Alert at Saumur

Year after year the cadet officers under instruction at Saumur would be made to play the same war-game. The theme of the game was a threat to the Cavalry School posed by an advancing enemy. The examination question would begin: 'After a number of unfortunate engagements north of the Loire, a friendly side is retreating to the south protected by a division of cavalry deployed along the front from Gennes to Montsoreau....' The pupils would then be required to organize the defence of this sector of the river, from Gennes in the west to Montsoreau in the east, a front of some forty kilometres, with Saumur and its Cavalry School somewhere in the middle.

In June 1940 the exercise, made familiar over the years, ceased to be a game and, with some modifications, became reality. In the real war that was approaching Saumur, the '*parti ami*', the friendly side, was but the scattered and disorganized remnants of the French armies that, having survived the battles on the Seine and along the Aisne, were trying to put the Loire between themselves and the enemy; nor was there any cavalry division to support them, as in the war-game, along the front from Gennes to Montsoreau.

This was the precise sector of the river that the Commandant of the Cavalry School, Colonel Michon, had undertaken to defend after General Weygand's general instruction to prepare the defences of all the rivers that might bar the German advance to the south. However, all that had been envisaged at first was to counter possible raids by marauding German columns intent on provoking panic among the civilian population, causing them to flee, to block the roads and in general hamper French military resistance. Instructions referred merely to 'contingency defences, local and temporary'.

In the first week of June, therefore, Colonel Michon prepared the defence of the bridges between Gennes and Montsoreau, as they had always been defended in the war-game, and relays of cadets provided a twenty-four-hour watch and night patrols along the roads. No one, not even the Commandant, really believed that the Cavalry School would ever have to be anything more than the educational establishment it had always been. Surely, it was argued, remnants of the Cavalry, such as Colonel du Vigier's men of the 3rd Light Mechanized Division at nearby Fontevrault, would never have been brought back into the area to be re-formed after their losses, if there had been any real risk of the war reaching the Loire?

At the Cavalry School, despite the special arrangements about the watches on the bridges and the night patrols, classes continued as usual. Books were read, lessons were prepared, instruction was given. More time was now being spent on the weapons range, the instructors concentrating on teaching their charges the proper use of arms, automatic rifles, machine-guns, mortars, anti-tank weapons and whatever ancient piece of artillery they could lay hands on.

Ever since their arrival at Saumur the cadets had had but one idea, to get into the fighting as soon as possible, to complete their training course and be posted to a cavalry regiment at the front. That the front was in fact coming to them was something that took a long time to penetrate. At first the preparations along the river front seemed more like an extension of the war-games than their initiation into the war itself. None had yet heard a shot fired in anger, though all were keen to do so. Young Jean-Louis Dunand, who had given up his architectural studies at the *École des Beaux Arts* in Paris to become a cavalry cadet at Saumur, wrote to his parents: 'I am so impatient to be in the fight, as are all my comrades here. Times a hundred times more painful await me but I am prepared to meet them with a smile.' Those, it seemed, were also the sentiments of their Commandant.

Colonel Daniel Michon was an old warrior who had campaigned in Morocco in 1907 in the *Chasseurs d'Afrique* under one of Saumur's great men, Marshal Lyautey, taking part in the battle of Benisnassen. During the Great War, like many other cavalry officers, he had volunteered to fight with the infantry and in 1915 had been severely wounded in the trenches at Calonne near St-Mihiel. For two days he lay under a mound of corpses until rescuers dug him out. His wounds had never healed properly; he was very often in pain and, when war broke out in September 1939, active service at the front was out of the question. All his love for the Army, all his devotion to its ancient ideals, were now concentrated on making its officers of tomorrow from the ardent young men whom the War Department had entrusted to his charge. He had found a new vocation as a teacher who not only communicated successfully his own profound feelings of patriotism and his highly idealistic view of the role of the French officer in expressing all that was finest in the values of his country but in so doing was able to win the admiration and devotion of his young cadets.

Those who in April 1940 had been summoned back from their regiments to be instructors at Saumur, who had been at the top of their promotions of the previous four years and personally chosen by Michon, had been able to temper their disappointment at being pulled out of the line to the safety of Saumur by a sense of loyalty to their Commandant. Among these was Jacques Desplats, aged twenty-eight, at whose marriage the best man had been a certain Captain de Hautecloque who, as General Leclerc, was to become one of France's heroes of the Second World War. Among their colleagues were their friends the Comte de Galbert and Gérard Liffort de Bufféevent, both of whom had lost their fathers killed in action in the First World War, and Raymond de St-Germain, Périn de St-André, the Comte de St-Pol, the Comte Martin de Marolles and Hubert de la Lance. Their very names demonstrate how the Cavalry School continued to attract an aristocratic élite, young men from noble families which the revolution of 1789 and subsequent upheavals had failed to destroy and who continued to follow from generation to generation the military traditions established by their ancestors in battles long ago along the Loire. 'In them', commented Colonel Michon, 'I have the finest soldiers from the front.' If I have to defend the Loire, if I have to defend the School itself from the enemy, then, thought Michon, these are my chosen lieutenants. With them he set to work, following General Pichon's instructions, to organize the defence of his sector and to adapt the routine of the school to meet the latest developments in the war.

The roads beside the forty-kilometre stretch of the Loire going west from Gennes (a hamlet which is today 'twinned' with Wincanton in Somerset) to Montsoreau in the east, with Saumur between them, Colonel Michon's front in June 1940, are among the best-known of the routes that criss-cross that region of France, known as 'the Château Country of the Loire' and which every summer attract tourists in their thousands. There are four places at which the river can be crossed: over the bridges at Gennes and Montsoreau at each end of the sector, at Saumur itself and towards Montsoreau again at the viaduct carrying the railway line from Bordeaux to Paris.

Gennes and Saumur each have two bridges to cross, since in the river opposite each of these places is an island. The Pont Cessart links the centre of Saumur to its 'suburb' of Offard Island, and from the island to the north bank of the river is the bridge known in 1940 as the Pont Napoléon and today as the Pont des Cadets. At Gennes a much smaller island is linked to each of the river banks by suspension bridges. On the north bank, facing Gennes, is the little village of Les Rosiers with its ancient church on the little square where stands a statue of its benefactress, Jeanne de Laval, wife of King René the Good and stepmother of an English Queen, Marguerite, the wife of Henry VI. All these bridges were the strategic points that the Cavalry School was to defend. It was, of course, familiar ground, since it was part of that war-game that successive cadet courses had been playing for years at Saumur.

The Chief Instructor at Saumur was Commandant Lemoyne, Colonel Michon's 'major' and, after the fighting began, his Chief of Staff. Together they divided up their 780 pupils, some 200 of whom, being Service Corps cadets, had never been intended as fighting personnel, into twenty-eight brigades,* each commanded by an instructor lieutenant. Five brigades were then gathered together to make a squadron.

The squadrons and, indeed, most of the brigades were commanded by much older men than the dozen instructors, still in their twenties, whom Michon had had sent back from the front. These were officers of the Cavalry Reserve, some of whom had served in the First World War, men such as the

* A brigade in France is a small unit under instruction.

indomitable Captain Foltz, whose squadron included Lieutenant de Galbert's brigade, Captain de St-Blanquat and Captain Marzolf. There were some unusual officers, such as Lieutenant Lucien Fraisse, who was a Jesuit priest who had temporarily forsaken the cloth for his old Cavalry uniform and returned to Saumur as an instructor. He took command of the 15th Brigade. According to one of the cadets, he was a powerfully built man with a massive head; somewhat austere, laughing rarely, he went about his duties with a resolute air. And there was Commandant de Launay, twice decorated in the First World War, who in 1940 was mayor of Vendôme; he, too, had put on his old uniform and returned to Saumur, as the military situation became ever more threatening.

Events were beginning to overtake them with a disconcerting rapidity. Early on the afternoon of 13 June General Weygand had ordered the general retreat of the French armies; the German Panzers were over the Seine and the Marne; during the night of 13/14 June Paris had been abandoned; the Government had been at Tours since the 10th, and on the 14th withdrew once more to Bordeaux. As Lieutenant de Galbert had suggested, that afternoon in the school courtyard, the Loire had become a major area of operations; it was France's last chance to stop the Germans along the natural defence line of a river.

However, with its thousand kilometres of water, the Loire does not cross the country in a straight line but moves in a wide loop towards the north. The Saumur sector, to the west of the loop, lies somewhere in the centre. The German advance had been swiftest on the flanks, in the west towards Normandy, in the east down to Dijon and beyond towards Lyons, and it was to prevent the encirclement of French troops in the centre (which might result from the Germans having forced the lower Loire and their deep encroachment via the upper Loire and the Allier rivers) that French troops had been ordered to move south as quickly as possible.

One of these retreating armies was the still intact 200,000-strong Army of Paris, commanded by the elderly General Héring who had been with General Sir William Rawlinson during the First World War. At the beginning of June Weygand had transferred him from his post as Military Governor of Paris to command this army while the Germans were still north of the capital. If the Army of Paris were to escape the German pincers, it was vital to hold the central Loire between Angers and Tours, and this was General Pichon's responsibility.

In delegating to the Cavalry School the task of defending a crucial part of this sector, the Saumur bridges, General Pichon knew the risk he was taking. The morale and patriotic zeal of its Commandant, Colonel Michon, his instructors and their pupils were beyond question, but a military academy, not being a fighting unit, was not part of the intricate and detailed organization that supports an army in the field in time of war; its Commandant has no part in the command structure of the general in charge of operations in the field. Colonel Michon had accepted with pride the military task assigned to the school in an hour of crisis but, being an experienced soldier he knew that, with the best will in the world, his school was simply not equipped to fight; he had neither the arms nor the munitions, not even a sufficient supply of food to maintain men in the field for any length of time. His general knew all this and was doing his utmost to help.

Having established his headquarters at Azay-le-Rideau, site of one of the finest of the Loire châteaux and near Colonel du Vigier's reassembling motorized cavalry, from whom he borrowed transport and telephones, since he had none, General Pichon was constantly on the move. At Tours he managed to get a few light tanks; from a driving school he requisitioned cars and motorcycles; at Poitiers the artillery promised him two batteries of 75 mm guns. But it was not until early on the morning of Saturday 15 June that one of his officers, Lieutenant Henri Lemaire, arrived at the imposing entrance to the Cavalry School at Saumur with a lorry piled high with material.

However, as General Pichon also realized, arms and stores were not all that the Commandant needed. According to the school textbooks, a proper defence of the Saumur sector would require some 80,000 men, several divisions; Colonel Michon, his instructors and their pupils numbered some 780. In due course, thanks to the efforts of his general and others, Colonel Michon eventually went into battle with 2,190 men.

They were a mixed lot. General Pichon sent him 200 Algerian riflemen from a training camp; these were divided into five groups of forty and sent to support each of the five cadet brigades manning the bridges. Other, more experienced soldiers reaching the Cavalry School also came under the command of Colonel Michon. Commandant Hacquard brought in a group of 260 cavalrymen, all that was left of several squadrons of the 19th Dragoons. Another group, 210 men, arrived with Captain de Neuchèze; this was a *groupe franc*, one of the freelance units operating independently, armoured and motorized, and carrying out daring raids behind enemy lines. Neuchèze had put together his little private army at Montlhéry on 17 May; from 21 May until 27 May they had fought on the Somme and the Seine. Having patched up his own four wounds at Rouen, he had brought his men with their five light Hotchkiss tanks and some armoured cars to Saumur and put himself at Colonel Michon's disposal.

Of the other groups that had been hurriedly put together, the biggest, 450 men under Lieutenant Cadignan, belonged to a training centre for mechanized warfare at Fontevrault. Another group was made up of men who had lost contact with their own units in the chaos in the north and, arriving at the Cavalry School, still had 'the taste for battle and the heart to fight'.

One day a small, battered vehicle pulled up outside the gates of the school; a soldier's head looked out. 'There are five of us,' he told the duty officer. 'We lost our unit coming back from Dunkirk but we want to fight. What shall we do? We've got munitions,' he said and produced a machine-gun. A place was found for them.

Such men were more often than not the exception. There were others in uniform lying about on the pavements, some of them sleeping off the effects of too much drinking. The wine of Anjou would make them aggressive, and they would begin to abuse those of their comrades who still wanted to fight, shouting at them to forget the imbecile war and to go home. The atmosphere in and around Saumur became increasingly confused, adding to the difficulties of the general who was trying to organize the defence of the central Loire and of the colonel who was particularly concerned with the protection of the town and of the Cavalry School whose Commandant he was.

If General Pichon had needed any reminder that it was no longer war-games but war itself that he was dealing with on the

Loire, it soon came. He had driven over to Chinon to consult with Colonel du Vigier and to arrange for a meeting at Tours the next morning of the various commanders along his sector. He arrived back at his quarters at four o'clock in the morning and had only just got into bed when his house was hit by a bomb from an enemy aircraft. Two hours later he was pulled out of the rubble by his regional chief, General Vary, and despite his injuries insisted on presiding over the meeting of his colonels, as arranged.

Pichon passed on what he knew of the situation. He had been in contact with General Héring in the east and impressed upon them what that general had told him about the importance of holding the central sector until the Army of Paris might be in a position to do what Joffre had done on the Marne in 1914, finally put a break on the German advance. Meanwhile, in the west General de la Laurencie's Third Corps had reached Angers, at the end of Pichon's sector, having lost contact with Tenth Army due to the speed of the German drive into Normandy and Brittany.

De la Laurencie had also lost Major-General Laurie's 52nd British Division, which had been under his command. Had Laurie been allowed to stay, British troops might well have taken part in that last defence of the Loire. While Weygand was still at Briare, General Sir John Dill, Chief of the Imperial General Staff, had offered him the use of British forces in France to employ as he saw fit. On 14 June General Alan Brooke, in command of those forces, having talked to Weygand, had decided that France's position was hopeless and advised Dill to pull his forces out of France. To his chagrin, General de la Laurencie had to part with his British contingent.

In time of peace, as de la Laurencie remembered from his own days at Saumur, the *École de Cavalerie* retained close relations with the British Cavalry; a British officer was always on liaison at Saumur, as he is today, and would sometimes ride in the Carrousel, as he did in 1984. But in mid-June 1940 France was alone when it went to meet its fate on the Loire. At the last moment a group of Polish officers in training at Saumur quit the Cavalry School for Cherbourg in order to sail with British troops returning home.

The ships at Cherbourg carrying the last of Britain's troops in

France cast off from the quays with the Germans only five kilometres from the docks. It was four o'clock on the afternoon of 18 June, and at that very moment the gates of the Cavalry School at Saumur closed behind the last of the cadets going to their battle stations up and down river.

The British had begun to withdraw from France on 15 June, a Saturday. On that day the French Government meeting in Bordeaux had reached a crisis of indecision about what France should do – seek an armistice or fight on from its North African empire. But in the Hôtel du Commandement at the Cavalry School at Saumur, Colonel Michon ignored the wider world and was concentrating on the task in hand, the defence of his school and of its river front, and how best to employ the motley collection of reinforcements he had received. Out at the bridges and on the islands at Gennes and Saumur his cadet brigades, he knew, were already adding to their defences; on Offard Island facing Saumur, Gérard de Buffévent was erecting anti-tank barricades, blocks of concrete facing the bridge, and finding a place for the ancient 25 mm gun with which in due course Cadet Paulin Houbé would perform wonders. On the island in the river between Gennes and Les Rosiers Lieutenant Jacques Desplats, his beloved Airedale, Nelson, always at his heels, was moving about in the undergrowth selecting positions for his machine-guns. From his window Colonel Michon could see down into the courtyard where Lieutenant Henri Lemaire was attending to the offloading of the lorry that he had brought in that morning. Then from Angers arrived sappers of the 6th Engineers who had been sent to mine all the bridges on Colonel Michon's sector, bridges which, as Michon knew all along, would inevitably have to be blown.

'The arrival of our lorries in Saumur took place in a particularly unnerving atmosphere,' wrote Sergeant Camille Thelinge with the party of sappers. 'Thousands of cars were passing over the bridges, and enemy aircraft flew incessantly over the town.' There was one alert after another, and every time there was an alert, the traffic stopped on the bridges while the terrified refugees piled up in the main streets as they sought shelter. Because of the traffic jams, Thelinge's group was an hour late getting to the railway viaduct. 'The cavalry cadets had established a guard post there and wondered what our arrival signified. They thought they had been sent reinforcements but we had to put them right, explaining that we had come to mine the railway viaduct.' They showed their orders to Lieutenant Hubert de la Lance commanding the 10th Brigade at the bridge and then went to work. 'It was a particularly arduous job,' Thelinge wrote, 'going from one end of the bridge to the other on the over-heated sheet-iron, under a burning sun in insupportable heat, with our helmets on our heads.' De la Lance watched them at work and was impressed. 'The officer commanding the guard post,' Thelinge noted, 'congratulated those in charge of our detachment several times on their fine turn-out. These congratulations coming from an instructor at the school, a lieutenant of Cuirassiers, particularly flattered the sappers and encouraged them to work even better.'

When Thelinge had to return to Saumur to get wood to make sleepers for the charges they were putting under the viaduct, he watched his fellow sappers working on the Saumur bridges linking Offard Island. They were constantly having to break off from their work in order to direct the traffic that was still pouring over the bridges – according to one account, a thousand vehicles an hour over the Pont Cessart. The refugees in their cars seemed unaware that the bridges they were crossing were having explosives placed under them. 'Some German prisoners passed,' recorded Thelinge, 'and people ran to look at them. As they looked as if they had just come out of battle, they were thought to be parachutists, but no, they were already of the advance guard since the enemy was much closer than we thought, barely 100 kilometres away from us and all the time we thought they were still at the Seine.' The lack of information, the break-down in communication, was becoming ever more apparent.

Such a day of activity at Saumur, at its Cavalry School, at the bridges guarded by its cadets, still being crossed by refugees while they were being mined by sappers, all under a burning sun and the constant attention of enemy aircraft – such a day was bound to have its dénouement. It came at five o'clock that afternoon.

The telephone rang in the Hôtel du Commandement at the Cavalry School. On the line was the Director of Cavalry at the War Ministry, which, since the Government's withdrawal from

Paris, was temporarily established at Vallière-les-Grandes about ninety kilometres to the east of Saumur. Colonel Michon could hardly believe what he was being told. He was stunned. He was being ordered to quit Saumur, to withdraw his entire school, staff, cadets, horses, everything they had, and go to Montauban in the south, miles away from the enemy. He was to send one of his staff officers immediately to Vallière to discuss with the Directorate of Cavalry detailed arrangements for the removal of the school.

Colonel Michon put down the telephone and exploded. 'It's impossible,' he shouted. 'The enemy will have to pass over my dead body rather than that I'll give way.'

After a while he regained his composure. 'I have an order to defend the Loire,' he told his staff firmly. 'The honour of the school is at stake.' It was perfectly reasonable, he agreed, that all the non-combatant elements at the school, the administrative and civilian staff, should withdraw to safety and take with them the files, the archives, the treasures of the school museum collected over the centuries, and of course the 800 horses which were France's pride and fortune, the riding school of the *Cadre Noir* and all its valuable equipment. Michon delegated one of his staff officers, Lieutenant de Gaillard de Lavaldène, to go to Vallière to see General Rupied, the Director of Cavalry, and to put to him as forcibly as he could his colonel's views. Together they worked out what should be said to the general, and before long de Gaillard de Lavaldène was on his way.

At 10.30 that evening General Rupied was listening to what he had to say. 'I come on behalf of Colonel Michon to say that the school cannot steal away as the Germans arrive on the Loire without betraying all its traditions,' de Gaillard was saying. He then went on to give more practical reasons. The departure of the school would leave a serious hole in the defences of the Loire, a vital forty-kilometre stretch of the river allotted to the school by General Pichon for whose defence they had been preparing busily. General Pichon, in the stress of the hour, had clearly ignored the fact that the Cavalry School was the responsibility neither of the *Grand Quartier-General* nor of the territorial command of the Ninth Military Region where it was situated geographically, but was the sole concern of the Director of Cavalry at the War Ministry. However, General Rupied was understanding. He agreed that the Colonel with his teaching staff and pupils, together with the personnel from the mechanized training centres already forming Lieutenant Cadignan's group of 450, should be temporarily detached to continue under General Pichon's overall command of the sector to defend the school. General Rupied had his staff officer put his new orders in writing, and these Lieutenant de Gaillard was to hand to Colonel Michon. He was also given new orders for Colonel Halter and Colonel de St-Laumer, who were in charge of the mechanized training centres from which Lieutenant Cadignan's men had come. It was made clear that, once the battle on the Loire was over, the Director of Cavalry would retrieve from General Pichon his former authority.

Armed with his letter, de Gaillard set off once more through the night. Driving along roads on which a stream of traffic was moving ceaselessly towards him, he made only slow progress. It was already beginning to get light by the time he reached Saumur and gave to Colonel Michon the news he had been anxiously awaiting. It was now Sunday 16 June.

Colonel Michon, meanwhile, had not been idle. Late the previous day he had summoned all his staff and the cadets to assemble in the grand amphitheatre of the school. None knew of the mission that Lieutenant de Gaillard de Lavaldène was undertaking. Michon was carrying on with his plans as if nothing had happened to disturb them.

'Gentlemen,' he told them, 'for the school it is a mission of sacrifice. France is depending on you.' * The course had been suspended, he told them; there would be no more classes. From now on, the school was on a permanent war footing; the squadrons and brigades would remain in formation indefinitely. Any further instruction would be given at battle stations.

Among the cadets there was immediate excitement and, after the assembly broke up, they began to question their instructors. Jacques Desplats came to speak to his men in their living-quarters. He looked grave. They had thought the enemy was

* Instructor Lieutenant Vladimir de Favitski of 17th Brigade, later General de Favitski, recorded: 'I can still hear him say, "We owe it to the honour of the Cavalry to defend the Saumur positions even if it makes no difference to the outcome".'

in Normandy somewhere, in the region of Lisieux. 'The enemy is at Chartres,' he told them. 'Anything can happen now. We've been given the job of defending the Loire. You've got an hour to get ready.'

There was a mood of exaltation; they could hardly believe their good fortune – as they saw it – that they were really going to do battle. Despite the air-raids they had witnessed, despite the pitiful stream of refugees through Saumur, and the lost and footloose soldiery sheltering at the school, these boy-soldiers, judging from the letters they wrote and the conversations that were recorded, had still not linked the reality of the war in France in June 1940 with their own often romantic notions of battle. After Desplats had left, the most enthusiastic among them suggested they should repeat the celebrated example of the young subalterns from St-Cyr who in 1914, in full dress uniform, plumed hats on their heads, white gloves on their hands, had charged the enemy with drawn swords. For the cadets of Saumur in June 1940, however, there would be no fancy dress. The discipline they had been taught demanded a degree of smartness in their turnout, as if they were about to go on parade in the Cours d'Iéna in the heart of the Cavalry School, properly buttoned and with shining boots – all that was normal – but only the distinctive black and red escutcheon on their battledress proclaimed, like an old school tie, their élite origins, the colours of the Cavalry School of Saumur. The example was set by their instructors. Captain Foltz, remarking on the impeccable appearance of Lieutenant the Comte de Galbert commanding his 27th Brigade, got a broad grin and a brave reply: 'What a good-looking corpse I'll make, *mon capitaine*!'

As they made their preparations, some of the cadets recalled what their instructor, Lieutenant Desplats, had said to them the previous day. 'You lack discipline', he had grumbled, dissatisfied with their performance under instruction. 'How do you expect to lead men if you yourselves have no discipline?' Within a few days Desplats demonstrated to them in dramatic and tragic example what he had meant.

Meanwhile there was time to get off a quick letter home. One of Desplats's men, eighteen-year-old Raymond Deutz d'Arragon, told his parents:

The Germans are advancing rapidly, very rapidly; this morning some of our motorized comrades went on ahead to make contact. In spite of our anxiety about what is going to happen to us, we are happy at the thought of being able soon to take part in trying to stop this frightful rout.

The Colonel commanding the school has held up a proclamation before us. We are now to be the Cadets of the Cavalry* and we must follow the example of our predecessors; there is of course no question of retreat.

What a terrible cavalcade passes before our eyes, refugees, soldiers, in cars, on bicycles, motorcycles, in ceaseless procession; if only this stampede could be stopped! This morning we finished our shelter for the machine-gun, a wonderful shelter, solid as a rock, protected from bullets and even shells, in fact a little marvel; it only remains to baptize it. I am the trigger man and will take my place in this charming little chalet at the water's edge with my two comrades, de Farcy and du Bellaing.

Now I must ask you to be good and not torment yourselves about me, even if something happens, do not be too upset – I shall have left this world with its twenty centuries of civilization with a smile and in thinking of you all.

Another cadet who wrote home that fateful weekend was the former architectural student Jean Dunand, a colleague of Raymond d'Arragon in Lieutenant Desplats's brigade defending the island at Gennes. It was the last letter he ever wrote. 'It will all work out,' he said. 'Setbacks are a part of victory; these could last five years or more but in the end it is the final result that counts.'

Sunday 16 June. At Bordeaux, before the day was out, Paul Reynaud, the Prime Minister, exhausted by the bickering, pessimism and defeatism of many of his Cabinet, surrendered his office to Lebrun, the President of the Republic, and France acquired in the eighty-four-year-old Marshal Pétain a new Head of Government. Supported by Commander-in-Chief General Weygand, who also became Defence Minister, he at once set in

* Many years later General Deutz d'Arragon, as he became, explained how as an eighteen-year-old pupil at Saumur in June 1940 he had used the expression 'Cadets of the Cavalry'. The word *cadet* had come from the Gascon *capdet*, itself derived from the Latin *caput*, and meant 'young leader'. In the days of the Gascon cadets, the young gentlemen of good family learned to become officers not from textbooks but from actually fighting battles.

motion the diplomatic machinery for an armistice with the Germans.

While France came closer to bringing the fighting to an end, at Saumur Colonel Michon was busy preparing to fight his first battle of the war. He wrote a letter, marked it 'secret' and sent it by messenger to the mayor of Saumur, Robert Amy, for whom the war had brought its own personal tragedy: he had just learned that his son had been killed in the north four days earlier. Colonel Michon's letter told him that, 'In the event of the enemy arriving in sight of Saumur, all the houses in the Place du Roi René and along the quays on the north bank of the island would have to be evacuated.' He further explained that he, Colonel Michon, would give the order to evacuate, or in an emergency his deputy Commandant Lemoyne. The letter added: 'I request you to notify this decision to the people concerned with all discretion possible, in order to avoid panic among the population. It is very possible, though, that it won't come to this.'

Mayor Amy already had his own official problems, trying to deal with the flow of refugees into his town which had added thousands to its population. The fine old municipal theatre had been turned into a reception centre but there was still not enough shelter for those requiring it; nor was there enough food – in particular, bread – although the bakeries were working night and day trying to keep up with demand. Mayor Amy was not at all sure that he and his fellow citizens wanted their ancient and historic city turned into a battlefield. Colonel Michon had already had to convince the Director of Cavalry, General Rupied, that he and his cadets had to fight a battle at Saumur to save the military honour of their school; during the next twenty-four hours he would also have to take on the mayor of Saumur.

Michon's first concern, however, was to procure arms, so that his little army might have something to fight with. That Sunday evening at six o'clock he presided over a meeting in the Hôtel du Commandement which was attended not only by senior officers such as Colonel Halter from the mechanized training centre at Fontevrault but by General Rupied's representative from the Directorate of Cavalry, Captain Troncsarrazin.

Colonel Michon had to battle to get the material he needed,

since General Rupied's man was insisting that the forces regrouping in the south urgently needed tanks and armoured cars which might fall into enemy hands if left on the Loire with the Commandant of the Cavalry School, whose battle could have only one result. In the end, however, Michon did not do too badly. Originally the school had had eighty-five automatic rifles, some ten machine-guns, some badly worn 25 mm guns, a few 60 mm and 81 mm mortars and three Panhard armoured cars that had seen service in the First World War and ever since had been used for instruction at Saumur. His force finally went into battle with thirty-five machine-guns, 110 automatic rifles, some of which had been new in 1915, ten 25 mm guns, four 81 mm mortars and seven 60 mm mortars, five small combat tanks, the Hotchkiss H39, three armoured cars, eight caterpillar transports and two 75 mm pieces of artillery – the latter so old that the Commandant had not dared to use them even for firing off blanks to salute the Fête Nationale on 14 July, Bastille Day.

Each of the cadets went to his battle station with a musket and 100 rounds of ammunition; some also had a revolver and hand grenades. According to their teaching, their river front for its proper defence against an enemy in force required 2,000 automatic rifles, 800 machine-guns, 300 mortars and a squadron of tanks. However, the time for textbooks had passed. That popular French military expression *'Débrouillez-vous'* – 'Make the best of it' – was now constantly in use at Saumur and had been part of Colonel Michon's vocabulary even since the start of the emergency. And so, indeed, they would when the time came.

The initial euphoria among the cadets had now been overtaken by determination and resignation. That Sunday afternoon, when some of them were talking in the school courtyard, Lieutenant de Galbert was there, and a civilian who was a retired colonel recalled the occasion later. 'The game is lost,' one of the cadets was saying, 'but we're still here and we'll do some good work before we fall.' The civilian had been speaking to him about the future, about what he would do when peace returned. 'Don't count on me,' the cadet had said with a brave smile. Later, as the visitor was leaving, de Galbert went to see him off. 'Yes, they're fine,' he was saying. 'That's why I like them. Tomorrow I shall be putting myself at their head.' Then, pausing for a moment, he added, 'But I'm afraid it will be to lead them to a sacrifice.'

All about them everything was changing. The school looked as if it were packing up not just for the holidays but for ever. Military vehicles were being loaded up with boxes of documents and files, with everything that belonged to the administrative service. Colonel Michon was carrying out his orders to evacuate all personnel who were neither instructors nor cadets, and everything that ought not to fall into the hands of the enemy. He had ordered his second-in-command, Lieutenant-Colonel Massiet, to see to the evacuation and to take the long convoy to Montauban when it was ready to go.

'I would prefer to stay and fight', Massiet had said.

'As second-in-command,' Michon had insisted, 'it is your job to organize the withdrawal. When can you leave?'

'Tuesday morning,' Massiet said bleakly.

Massiet was also ordered to take the standard of the Cavalry School. 'I entrust its safety to you personally,' Colonel Michon told him. The Colours – that precious military symbol providing a mystique respected by soldiers of all nations throughout history – could on no account be allowed to fall into enemy hands. In 1922 War Minister Maginot (he who gave his name to the Maginot Line) had come to Saumur to pin the *Légion d'Honneur* to the Colours in recognition of the part played by the men of Saumur in the Great War, and he had spoken of 'the traditional virtues of the French Cavalry, daring, fearlessness, the spirit of enterprise and sacrifice'.

Colonel Massiet had to take not only the Colours but also all the other symbols of the Cavalry School's historic past, the contents of the school's Barbet de Vaux museum. These included such historic relics as the cutlasses pitted with shot that had been carried by Colonel de Lacarre and Colonel de Beaune in the charge at Reichshoffen during the Prussian war of 1870, when both officers had been killed; the sabres of Marshal Kellerman, Marshal Comte Ornano and General Lasalle, and the Arabian cloak of the legendary Captain de Bournazal. Few of those who worked feverishly in the heat, piling up the lorries with these ancient relics of Saumur's past heroes, could have imagined that a new generation of such heroes was about to be created, that four or five names among those who were their own comrades that June day in 1940 would become part of the Saumur legend, that their relics, too, a sword, a tunic, a kepi, would find a place in that same museum, commemorating a new chapter in the history of the Cavalry School that was already beginning as they worked.

Loading lorries to evacuate men and material not required for action was one thing; preparing to remove 800 horses with a minimum of experienced riders was another. Colonel Massiet would have overall command of the convoy, both motorized and mounted, but the safe evacuation of the horses had been entrusted to another lieutenant-colonel who also happened to be one of France's most celebrated horsemen of the 1930s. Sunday afternoon found Colonel de Laissardière and his men hard at work in the stables of the riding school. All the special regalia of the *Cadre Noir*, the ceremonial harness and saddlery made familiar over the years at the annual Carrousel and at international riding events, had to be packed up and mounted on the trucks. Fodder, enough for a long march, had to be provided. Service Corps personnel worked throughout the night but there was not enough transport for everything that had to be removed.

Early on Monday morning, 17 June, more horses arrived at Saumur to join Colonel de Laissardière's convoy – those from a camp at Verrie had been brought in by men who had never rubbed down a horse, let alone ridden one. Another fifty horses, some of them riding mounts, others belonging to the artillery, came in from La Flèche. Departure for the mounted column was fixed for six o'clock the following morning, Tuesday 18 June. Some of the men at the Colonel's disposal had never ridden before; not only would they have to stay in the saddle, they would have to lead another horse at the same time. In the event some of them preferred to walk and to lead the horses behind them. It was not a promising prospect. The motorized column with Colonel Massiet would give them a five-hour start and then follow slowly behind.*

* It was decided that the horses of the Belgian royal family that had been at Saumur since 16 May should remain behind. They were left in the Cavalry School stables in the care of civilian grooms. When the Germans eventually entered Saumur, the horses were quickly dispersed to local farmers. King Leopold's personal horse, which he rode on ceremonial occasions, spent the

While the horses were coming into the stables at Saumur, on the airfield at Bordeaux a British aircraft was preparing to take off. Churchill's representative with Paul Reynaud, General Sir Edward Spears, was preparing to depart. Reynaud was no longer Prime Minister; Marshal Pétain had taken over and had already asked the German Government for its armistice conditions. Spears' mission was over. Or almost. At the last minute the tall, lean figure of General de Gaulle appeared by the aircraft as if he had come out to say goodbye. Suddenly a hand shot out and he was hauled on board the aircraft as it began to move down the runway. It had all gone according to plan.

De Gaulle's activities in London to keep France in the war were not to the liking of Pétain and Weygand, who wanted an end to hostilities, and he was expecting to be arrested by the new Government. The previous evening he had seen the British Ambassador, Sir Ronald Campbell, and told him of his wish to go back to London. He then asked Roland de Margérie, who had been head of Reynaud's office and was a distinguished ambassador, 'to send without delay to my wife and children, who were at Carentec, the passports they needed to reach England, which they just managed to do on the last boat leaving Brest'. He then concluded with Spears his arrangement to fly to London with him the next morning.

'We flew over La Rochelle and Rochefort,' de Gaulle recorded later. 'In the ports burned the ships, set on fire by German aircraft. We passed over Paimpont where my mother was, very ill. The forest was full of smoke from the munition depots that were being destroyed by fire.' After a short stop in Jersey, they flew on to London, reaching the capital early in the afternoon. De Gaulle went to the French Embassy, which he found extremely reserved and reticent in regard to himself. 'It seemed to me that I was alone and deprived of everything, rather like a man at the edge of a sea that he intends to swim across.'

If the French Embassy in London had been noncommittal, it had good reason to be: since lunchtime that day they were

---

next four years with a local dairyman who used it to deliver milk in the town during the German occupation. In 1945 motor transport arrived at Saumur from the Court in Brussels to fetch the horses.

probably wondering where they stood, wondering what was happening at home in France. At the Cavalry School at Saumur there was also confusion and dismay, which were dispelled only by the vigorous response of its Commandant, Colonel Michon, to the new situation that had arisen.

At 12.30 p.m. over the radio from Bordeaux had come the thin, pathetic voice of a very old man. It was that of the new Prime Minister, Marshal Pétain, who was addressing an important message to the nation.

> At the call of the President of the Republic, I am assuming as from today the direction of the Government of France. Sure of the affection of our fine army which struggles with a heroism worthy of its long military traditions against an enemy superior in numbers and arms, certain that, by its magnificent resistance, it has fulfilled its duty in regard to our allies, sure of the spirit of our veterans whom I had pride in commanding, sure of the confidence of all our people, I make to France the gift of my person to help reduce its misfortune. In these sad days I think of the unfortunate refugees who, completely destitute, trail along our roads. It is with a torn heart that I tell you that the fighting must cease. I have this past night been in touch with the enemy to ask him if he is ready with us, as soldiers, after the struggle and honourably to seek ways to end hostilities.

For the majority of Frenchmen, millions of whom were homeless refugees fleeing southward before the German advance, no doubt it was a relief to hear the voice of their old hero, Marshal Pétain, promising them peace; for millions of Frenchmen the war was being fought for no clear reason, and in any case it was lost. If the Victor of Verdun, their past hero, was speaking to them in this way, echoing the feelings of so many of them, then their lack of interest in the war, their defeatism, could be tolerated without too much of a conscience. As German propaganda posters, showing Pétain's photograph, soon would say to them: 'Are you more French than he?'

However, for other Frenchmen, who in the days ahead would be personified by General de Gaulle himself, Pétain's wavering voice was not the voice of the true France, and his broadcast had only served to underline the existence at a moment of historical crisis of two Frances, the one very different from the other. To that smaller group that owed allegiance to an older set of values that had apparently been lost in the France of the inter-war period, belonged the Cavalry School of Saumur, its Commandant, his instructors and their cadets. Some of them heard the broadcast in the mess, others at their posts at the bridges. 'It was over,' one of them wrote later. 'We saw ourselves lost, thrown off balance, diminished, hands and hearts empty. My comrade de C ... who was to die several days later, wept with rage as he threw his rifle to the ground.'

At a little farmhouse adjoining his post at one of the bridges, a cadet was being given a midday meal by the elderly woman of the house. She told him about the Marshal's broadcast and that it was going to be repeated at 13.30. He then ran back across the bridge to alert his comrades, and together they all went to a nearby inn to listen. The widow of one of those who died in the fighting at Saumur later recorded in a letter to her family: 'The people who ran this house told me that they all wept on listening to the voice of the old soldier. Only they themselves [the cadets] maintained a face of stone. When the Marshal had finished, the cadets were heard to say, ' "Never, we'll never retreat. We'll die here. They'll never get by." '

Colonel Michon had also heard the broadcast by Marshal Pétain, whose name was honoured by a staircase in the school buildings. As far as Michon was concerned, nothing had changed, the armistice had not been signed, France was still at war. The advance of the Germans had to be resisted. That was a soldier's duty; it was also a matter of honour. In Michon's philosophy, an army did not surrender: it fought on until it was annihilated. In such circumstances the honour of a French officer required that he get himself killed as valiantly as possible.

If Michon had taught such a philosophy to his cadets in their short time at Saumur, his success as a teacher was to be amply proved in the days that followed. One of his favourite instructors, Jacques Desplats, had tried to explain these things to his wife in a letter written soon after the war had started the previous September: 'It is our job to suffer and even to die in war, and my great hope is that you will understand this. The sacrifice of one's life is not something that counts for an active service officer, and his wife ought to have the necessary courage to bear this adversity. Continue to be courageous and optimistic and, if misfortune comes, I would wish you to keep a memory of your husband that was not sad but one full of dynamism, ardour, the will to fight.' After the combat at Saumur, Madame Desplats was to read that letter again and again.

Colonel Michon did not wait long after the Pétain broadcast before reassuring the cadets what he had decided to do. He was fully aware of the effect the broadcast had had on them. As Benoist-Méchin, a former minister, noted in his diary of those times, the Marshal's words had coursed through their veins like fire-water. Some of them had begun to raise their voices. 'Are we going to fight,' they were demanding, 'or are we just going to hand over this place to the Germans, run away, accept the irreparable without doing anything?' They heard the Commandant's announcement with relief. 'Good! the decision's taken.' And they cheered. 'We're going to fight,' and then the inevitable '*Vive la France*.'

Colonel Michon had made his decision: he had completed his plans for the defence of the school and the Saumur sector and had already dispatched a cadet brigade under Lieutenant Garnier across the river to carry out a reconnaissance towards La Flèche and Noyant to try to find out what the enemy was doing.

But the Colonel had failed to reckon with the Mayor and his town council. If an armistice was coming, they argued, why should they endanger the lives of their fellow citizens and risk the destruction of their historic town? In any case, the Government at Bordeaux had already announced that towns with populations of more than 20,000 would not be defended and would be declared 'open'. In normal times Saumur did not have such a large population but, since there were now thousands of refugees in the town, it had many more than 20,000 people. The Mayor was confident there would be no fighting at Saumur, and soon he had one of his men patrolling the streets with a loud-hailer telling the citizens they had nothing to worry about, that Saumur would soon be declared an open city.

A confrontation between the Cavalry School and the town of Saumur was now inevitable. Colonel Michon immediately dispatched a messenger to the town hall with a letter, and Mayor Amy read as follows: 'I have the honour to have been charged with the defence of Saumur and of a sector of the Loire. I know

I can count on your devotion and your patriotism and that you will support my efforts in the defence of Saumur.' The Mayor tried to reason with the Commandant of the Cavalry School and asked Monsieur Cruveilhier, a deputy prefect normally stationed at Nantes, already declared an open city, to go and see the Colonel. Michon told him firmly that the honour of the Cavalry School was at stake and that the school would 'resist to the death'.

The next morning, Tuesday 18 June, the Mayor made another last attempt to save his town from battle, when, after the council had met, he telephoned to military headquarters at Tours, where Michon's ultimate superior, the General commanding the Ninth Region, had his office. General Vary himself was on the other end of the line but could offer the Mayor no comfort.

'I cannot change the orders,' he said. 'I have to take account of the Government's decree concerning open cities which has been published in the Press.'

'Well, then, General,' the Mayor persisted, 'if Saumur is to be defended, allow me to evacuate the population.'

'No,' said General Vary. 'Saumur will be defended and will not be evacuated.' And he put down his receiver.

Soon after this the Mayor received confirmation in a message from Bordeaux brought to him via Angers: 'Any evacuation of the public service or the civil population is forbidden; to this effect take every measure to keep the population where it is and prevent any departure, particularly by car. Punishment will be meted out on the spot to any public authorities contravening this order.'

Once more the local electrician, Monsieur Barrault, driving the car with the loud-hailer, went round the town informing its citizens that they were to remain at Saumur and warning them that, if they abandoned their homes, these might well be requisitioned. The Mayor, now that the die was cast and he and his fellow citizens had to stay to witness a battle, was determined to do all he could to protect his people. Some, particularly those with cars, had left the previous day as for the first time they sensed the danger that was approaching.

At five o'clock the next morning, Tuesday 18 June, the Saumur telephone exchange received a call from the post office

Lieutenant-Colonel von Edelheim who led one of the German advance columns to Saumur

Major-General Kurt Feldt commanded the German cavalry against the Cadets of Saumur in June 1940, by which time both his young soldier sons had been killed in the war

Before their battle could begin, the cadets had to divert the endless refugee traffic from Saumur

18 June 1940 – the cadets leaving for their battle stations in trucks, as sketched at the time by Cadet Geoffroy de Navacelle

Colonel Daniel Michon, Commandant of the Cavalry School

Instructor Lieutenant Jacque Desplats died with his Airedal Nelson, as he defended the islan at Gennes

at Longué to say the Germans were approaching La Flèche. By noon the Mayor had got as many people as he could off the island, as Michon had requested in his first letter. Lieutenant Gérard de Bufféent with his 12th Brigade was already at his command post on the island, the premises of Boret, the grain merchant, near the bridge to the north bank, which was the most likely arrival point for the Germans. The town's Civil Defence workers, distinguished by a white armband, were busy shepherding men, women and children into the vast caves and natural wine cellars which abound at Saumur and where its famous sparkling wines are stored. Camp beds, blankets and food were brought in as if for a siege. Not all the sick from the hospital could be transferred to towns and villages south of the Loire; those who remained had to be carried into the wine cellars on stretchers, even on the backs of Civil Defence personnel. These included a wounded German airman.

Monsieur Roussel, in charge of the gas station, emptied the gasometers and turned off the taps. Shopkeepers closed their premises and boarded them up. People disappeared off the streets. Members of the territorial guard, summoned to the police barracks, were disbanded and told to go home for fear that if the town were invaded they might be taken for snipers. The local force of *gendarmes*, which the previous evening had been ordered to stay at its station, received a counter-order and took the road to the south.

At three o'clock in the afternoon Hubert de la Lance and his 10th Brigade at the railway viaduct saw the last train go by. They had grown used to the sight of the enormous Super Pacific locomotives drawing truck after truck, carrying not only munitions but refugees in uncovered waggons, among them the wounded who, as the train moved slowly over the mined bridge, would ask pitifully for water and food. Later they heard how a detachment of the German Light Infantry – the *Voltigorinfanter-isten* – had stopped the traffic higher up the line towards Tours, holding a train that carried fuel as well as refugees. The train had been shunted into a siding at Varennes-sur-Loire, and its crew and passengers were prisoners at the station.

No more trains. But still the roads leading to Saumur were crammed with refugees trying to make for the Loire bridges – cars, trucks, horse-drawn carts, wheelbarrows, hearses from funeral parlours, fire-engines from towns abandoned in the north, all carrying their pitiful human baggage. If these were allowed to cross the bridges and infiltrate Saumur, the defence of the town by the Cavalry School would have become impossible. The first task for the cadets, therefore, was to clear the battlefield of unwanted spectators before the arrival of their adversary. For these ardent young Frenchmen it was a disagreeable task, since they were constantly insulted and jeered at by their compatriots, many of them in uniform. Traffic had to be diverted to attempt crossings elsewhere; sometimes a senior officer had to be persuaded by an instructor lieutenant to abandon his car and continue his journey on foot.

The smart appearance of the cadets and their officers, in marked contrast to the unbuttoned and dishevelled uniforms of some of the fleeing soldiery, seemed to provoke insult. Lieutenant Jacques Desplats at Gennes, trying to persuade a vehicle crammed with fifteen desperate-looking men to take the road to Angers, received a torrent of abuse. 'Puppet,' jeered one of them. 'Push off.' The Lieutenant, according to one of his cadets recounting the incident later, turned very pale but with an astonishing self-control continued with his disagreeable duty; the vehicle, accelerating suddenly, shot off in the indicated direction.

On Tuesday 18 June, while Lieutenant Périn de St-André and his cadets of the 8th Brigade were reinforcing their defences with an anti-tank gun in the square opposite Saumur town hall, another behind a statue and a machine-gun in the bushes of Monsieur Hutrel's garden, the sight of such preparations for battle was too much for some of those still about in the streets, and they protested vigorously.

'You're going to fight, but why, why? Saumur will be made an open city, they've asked for an armistice, and you're going to get us all massacred, our houses bombarded and all to no purpose.'

To such words of good sense, the cadets had no reply. A soldier had to obey orders. That had been the first thing they had learned at Saumur. In any case, they had by now worked themselves up to such a pitch of nervous anticipation of combat that any kind of dialogue with anyone outside the army could have cracked their resolve. All the drama, all the pity of these last hours at Saumur, emphasized the agony of a nation that, having lost the war with Germany was now at war with itself. It was understandable that crowds of Frenchmen in the despair and misery of flight should be goaded by the sight of other young Frenchmen who were trying to help them into areas away from combat, and that in Saumur itself there were those who were ready to accept the enemy in their midst rather than that bright young men in smart uniforms should fight a battle there for the honour of their school or, as they believed, for France itself. But had France lost a war or only a battle?

At six o'clock that same evening of 18 June, by which time a strange silence had settled on the streets of Saumur, there was a voice speaking for France which, had the young cadets been able to hear it, would surely have compensated for the abuse and discouragement they had had to endure from some of their countrymen for whom they were about to sacrifice their lives. At that hour in a BBC studio General de Gaulle was broadcasting his historic message. 'Whatever happens,' he was saying, 'the flame of France's resistance must not and shall not be extinguished. The last word – has it been spoken?' he was asking. 'Must hope disappear? The defeat – is it permanent?' Then he thundered his own reply: 'No!' And he made his own declaration of French duty: 'All Frenchmen who are still carrying arms have the absolute duty to continue the resistance. Soldiers of France, wherever you are, arise!' At that hour on the 18th he might have been speaking to the Cadets of Saumur themselves, as he himself was later to recognize. His historic proclamation, the Appeal of 18 June, was directed '*A tous les français*'. The words of the appeal, fixed in a plaque, are there for everyone to read on the outer wall of 4 Carlton Gardens in London, where de Gaulle established the headquarters of the Free French. '*La France a perdu une bataille*,' one reads, '*mais la France n'a pas perdu la guerre*' – 'France has lost a battle but France has not lost the war.'

If the cadets of Saumur had received scant encouragement from some of their compatriots as they prepared to challenge on the Loire the might of the German Army, offering it the first resistance since its victorious crossing of the Seine, then the same could be said of General de Gaulle at the beginning of his historic mission in London. Each of them on that 18 June was making an act of faith.

Early that same morning the German 1st Cavalry Division, destined by pure chance to be the adversary of France's cavalry cadets, set off from Illiers, just south of the cathedral city of Chartres, to lead the assault on Saumur – which, as every German cavalryman knew, was the cradle of the French Cavalry, the site of its renowned Cavalry School against whose *Cadre Noir* some of their own officers had competed in Berlin the previous year.

These officers were the product of German's equivalent of Saumur, the Wehrmacht's cavalry school at Hanover. There, as at Saumur, a long aristocratic tradition continued to provide officers from the old landed nobility in Germany from the families of East Prussia, a region which had for generations bred and trained horses. By 1939 the 1st Cavalry Brigade was the last and only mounted unit of the German Army still in existence. The rank of Cavalry General had survived the advent of Hitler and the Nazis, and the German Cavalry continued to be regarded as an élite corps – the *arme d'élégance*, as the French described their own cavalry. It produced some of the most successful leaders in armoured warfare. During the fighting in France in June 1940 General von Kleist was the senior Cavalry General; as part of General von Rundstedt's Army Group South, he commanded Panzers with great distinction. With one or two exceptions, the Cavalry Generals represented all that was best in the German Army, and few of them emerged from the war with anything but credit.

The regiments of the 1st Cavalry Brigade, which by June 1940 had become the 1st Cavalry Division commanded by General Kurt Feldt, were the direct descendants of the old cavalry regiments of the Prussian Army. They had an *esprit de corps* and a cohesion that were highly developed, almost more so among the non-commissioned officers than among the officers, though the latter often represented a succession of father to son in the same regiments. The men in the ranks, all volunteers, were recruited from the rural communities of East Prussia, and these country people were noted for their discipline, tenacity and bravery in battle. The officer corps was less regional, except for the reserve officers, and at the outbreak of war their arrival for duty in large numbers from their country estates meant that the proportion of aristocratic officers in the mounted cavalry was considerably higher than in the other cavalry units, using tanks and armoured cars. As many of the German officers leading the cavalry attack on Saumur had the aristocratic tell-tale 'von' in front of their names as the French instructors and their cadets had the similar tell-tale particle 'de', 'de la' or 'du' in front of theirs.

General Dr F.M. von Senger und Etterlin, in 1983 Commander-in-Chief Allied Forces Central Europe, in his history of the 1st Cavalry Division, later the 24th Panzer Division, writing of the role of the horse in the training of cavalry, could have been speaking for Saumur as much as for Hanover when he maintained: 'It helps to create a sense of responsibility and a solicitude for the welfare of men; it stimulates pride and creates an harmonious balance between altruism and egoism which one finds among all men.' It was perhaps not without significance that in selecting Lieutenant St-Germain's squadron of five brigades for the defence of the bridges, Colonel Michon had chosen all those cadets who had been training at Saumur as mounted cavalry, the rest having been motorized from the beginning of their course.

The German Cavalry Division under General Feldt had operated as mounted troops with great success in the Polish campaign, in particular in the Pripet marshes, where tanks could not go, and in protecting the flanks of General Guderian's armoured group, as well as maintaining an important link between von Bock's Army Group North and von Rundstedt's Army Group South. It was to prove the most successful horse cavalry formation used extensively during the Second World War. Fresh from its success in Poland and converted from brigade to division with the addition of horse artillery, motorized units, battalions of cyclists and a communications section, the division had played an active part in the Low Countries and on 20 May reached Amiens in time to take part in the battle of the Somme. It crossed the Seine on 14 June and by 17 June was encamped at Illiers, south of Chartres.

At this point the Division, after its lengthy journeying and the tough fighting which had cost it dearly on the Somme, expected to be relieved and pulled out of the line. However, during the night its commanding officer was summoned to Army Group headquarters at La Potérie, where he received orders to march on Saumur and establish a bridgehead on the Loire. Anti-tank units and two artillery groups as well as infantry assault troops were attached to the division to facilitate its task. The German intention, now that their forces in the west and in the east were well down south into France, was to catch up in the centre; this meant they would have to move quickly to cover some 200 kilometres to the Loire between Angers and Tours, secure the bridges if possible but in any case get their forces across the river and go after the French armies that were pulling back along the central front.

The Cavalry Division was to spearhead the German advance, and to this end General Feldt dispatched three motorized columns, two of them commanded respectively by Lieutenant Colonel von Edelsheim and Lieutenant Colonel von Broich, making for Saumur by different routes and the third under Lieutenant Colonel Hoste aiming for Bourgueil and Port-Boulet to the east of Montsoreau bridge. The German mounted cavalry would follow later, after the motorized columns had cleared a way. So, in the end, the combat at Saumur was to be between cavalrymen on both sides, neither of whom had horses.

Whatever Hitler might decide to do about Marshal Pétain's request for the conditions of an armistice, as far as the German armies in France were concerned, the war was still being fought and they would pursue their object of bringing as much of France under their control as possible and destroying whatever resistance the French armies might still be able to offer. For the French armies, however, there was no such clarity of purpose. In fact, Pétain's broadcast at noon on 17 June had made their position even more confused. Some elements of the Army thought there had been an immediate cease-fire. During the afternoon General Georges had reported to Weygand that whole regiments were giving up. And from General Noguès, commanding French forces in North Africa, who had heard the Pétain broadcast and been deeply disturbed by it, had come a message seeking confirmation that resistance in France had ceased. Weygand replied forcefully: 'The Commander-in-Chief is astonished at the communication from General Noguès. The French troops are still resisting on all fronts in France.' And he immediately sent out orders to all commanders in the field to make sure that they were. He was to write later: 'During the two days of waiting [for a reply from the German Government] June 17 and 18 we were entirely absorbed in our very considerable tasks. My immediate preoccupations were concerned with our armies. How many days should we have to wait and meanwhile what would happen to our military situation? The German pursuit was meeting with weaker and weaker resistance.'

Weygand at this time was wearing two hats. As Defence Minister in the new French Government he was part of the civil authority that was seeking to end hostilities with an armistice; as Commander-in-Chief he was ordering his soldiers to continue fighting. As member of the civil power he could treat for peace with the enemy; as Commander-in-Chief he could not surrender – in his own words, 'the gravest crime which a commander can commit'. It was not surprising that the French Army, like the French Embassy in London, was confused about what was going on.

During the afternoon of 17 June the Pétain Government tried to correct the misunderstandings flowing from the Marshal's words 'I tell you we must stop the fighting'. It ordered the evening newspapers carrying the text of the broadcast to alter the sentence to 'We must try to stop the fighting.' And at 7.30 that evening Baudouin, who had stayed on in the new Government as Foreign Minister, also went on the air to declare that, despite the approach to the German Government for an armistice, France had 'not abandoned the struggle nor laid down arms'.

It was following this broadcast insisting that French resistance had to continue that the Mayor of Saumur received, first from General Vary, then from the Government at Bordeaux, the firm instruction that Saumur had to be defended. General Weygand in due course was also to refer to the confusion among mayors as to the defence of their towns:

> Many mayors [he wrote], fearing for their towns or owing to a misinterpretation of the message of 17 June inferring that hostilities had been suspended, succeeded in persuading the Cabinet, in accordance with the Government's wish to stop the exodus of populations by reassuring them as to the fate of their localities, to extend the specifying and safeguarding of towns declared to be open, to all those with not less than 20,000

> inhabitants. I had to accept these measures. But as I had not ceased to ask the troops to do all they could to hold back the enemy, I gave instructions that the defence of towns should be organized, if not on their outskirts or within them, at least a certain distance north or south of the inhabited areas.

Since the Loire was a natural line of defence and the last that stood between unoccupied France and the enemy, and as Saumur was situated on its banks, there could never have been any chance that Mayor Robert Amy's request would have been granted. But in any case by the morning of 18 June the need to hold the Germans at Saumur had become ever more pressing.

During the previous day General Besson's Third Army Group, which consisted of General Héring's Army of Paris together with the Seventh Army and the left flank of the Sixth Army, still had control of the loop of the Loire – that part of the river that stretches northward from Tours up towards Orleans and then southward again. But then the Germans got a foothold on the south bank at Briare where only four days earlier Churchill had met Weygand, and at Châtillon. This alarmed General Bresson, who then decided during the night of 18/19 June to move his forces from the Loire to the River Cher. At that moment, shortly after midnight, the 1st Cavalry Division, which had been moving up from near Chartres, to launch the German thrust in the centre, reached Saumur and the bridges they had been ordered to seize, where the Cadets of the Cavalry School were waiting for them.

Colonel Michon left the *École de Cavalerie* for the last time on the afternoon of Tuesday 18 June and, with his Chief of Staff, Commandant Lemoyne, and four other staff officers, drove along the Route des Crêtes along the heights past the château to their command post, the Villa des Grandes Brises, whose dining-room already had the businesslike look of an operations room. A telephone had been installed by the window which overlooked the broad stretch of the river below.

In Les Moulins, the villa behind the command post, three other officers had established a communications centre from which contact would be maintained with the various squadrons from the school and the other groups that had been assigned to

Colonel Michon for the defence of the sector. From here contact was also being maintained with the reconnaissance group under Lieutenant Garnier which, divided into three sections, had been moving about north of the river since Sunday and was covering the area La Flèche, le Mans and Tours, watching the approaches of the River Loir for any sign of the German advance.

On the Monday and early on Tuesday Garnier had reported his position as in the region of Château-du-Loir and Château-la-Vallière moving on Noyant. He was therefore right across the route that Colonel von Edelsheim and Colonel von Broich's motorized cavalry detachments had taken on leaving Illiers, near Chartres.

At four o'clock that afternoon of 18 June the last detachment to leave the Cavalry School, the cadet brigades of Captain de St-Blanquat's squadron, departed. Earlier Lieutenant de Galbert with his usual panache had reviewed his cadets, who, riding their motorcycles, had set off in perfect formation – and a roar of engines – to join Captain Foltz's squadron at Milly-le-Meugon on the road south from the Gennes bridges. Such was the display of boyish exhibitionism in their noisy departure that one of their fellows, Cadet de Changy, watching them go, exclaimed excitedly, 'A column of motorcyclists! Now that's really something!' It was difficult for them not to think that it was still a game to be enjoyed. With St-Blanquat's departure, Lieutenant Dufour, left behind as caretaker with one or two others, closed the great iron gates of the school, which, being now empty, had become suddenly and strangely silent.

It had been a perfect summer day, the hot sun blazing down hour after hour from a cloudless sky. The light faded only slowly, and when night came there was a bright moon to illuminate the countryside for miles around. Colonel Michon at his command post at the Villa des Grandes Brises had been surveying the river through his field-glasses, picking up the positions he had allotted to his men, going over in his mind again and again his plans for the defence of his sector. Looking westward where the river curved, he could still make out the tall fifteenth-century spire of the church of St-Eusèbe at Gennes, in front of which the road went in a straight line over the two suspension bridges across the island to Les Rosiers. Here

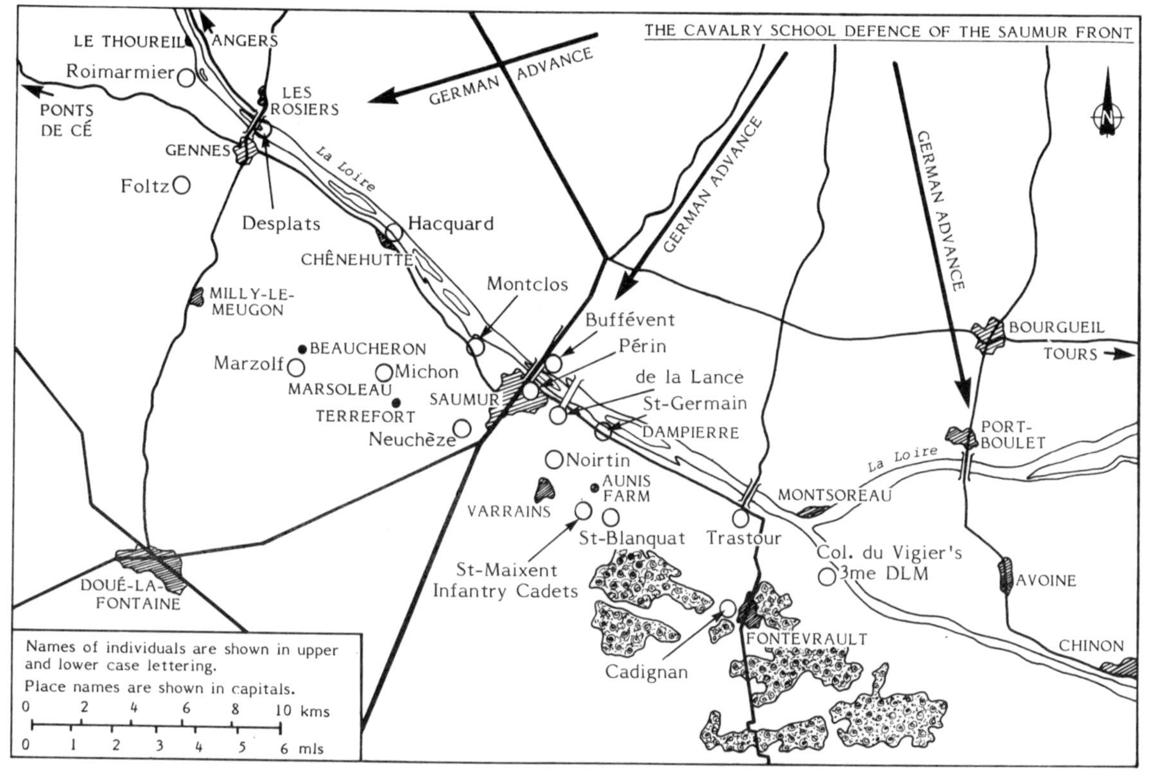
THE CAVALRY SCHOOL DEFENCE OF THE SAUMUR FRONT
LE THOUREIL
ANGERS
Roimarmier
PONTS DE CÉ
LES ROSIERS
GENNES
Foltz
La Loire
Desplats
Hacquard
CHÊNEHUTTE
GERMAN ADVANCE
GERMAN ADVANCE
GERMAN ADVANCE
MILLY-LE-MEUGON
Montclos
BEAUCHERON
Marzolf
Michon
MARSOLEAU
TERREFORT
SAUMUR
Neuchèze
Buffévent
Périn
de la Lance
St-Germain
DAMPIERRE
Noirtin
AUNIS FARM
VARRAINS
St-Blanquat
Trastour
St-Maixent Infantry Cadets
MONTSOREAU
La Loire
Col. du Vigier's 3me DLM
BOURGUEIL
TOURS
PORT-BOULET
AVOINE
CHINON
FONTEVRAULT
Cadignan
DOUÉ-LA-FONTAINE
Names of individuals are shown in upper and lower case lettering.
Place names are shown in capitals.
0 2 4 6 8 10 kms
0 1 2 3 4 5 6 mls

Jacques Desplats and the 11th Brigade, together with their Algerian riflemen, were waiting for the Germans in positions concealed by the trees and scrubs of the island. Some four kilometres to the west of the Gennes bridges and well out of range of Michon's glasses, were the 112 Service Corps cadets commanded by Lieutenant Jean-Pierre Roimarmier who were to support Desplats and somehow, despite their sparse numbers, fill the gap between Michon's sector and the 232nd Infantry Regiment belonging to General de la Laurencie's Third Corps at Angers. Jean-Pierre Roimarmier, a magnificent giant of a man, had, like Captain André Beaufre, spent much of his boyhood on the Loire. His grandfather had commanded the military school at La Flèche; his father, a veteran of Verdun, had been deputy prefect of the region, and as a boy Jean-Pierre had been at his side when he had inaugurated the new bridge at Gennes, which now his colleague Jacques Desplats was about to defend.

Training his glasses eastward again from Gennes, Michon could see the Château de Chênehutte where he had sent Commandant Hacquard and his men from the 9th Dragoons; in the undergrowth by the river they had parked their Hotchkiss tanks in readiness for action. Like Hacquart's group, another under Captain Montclos was trying to plug the gaps along the river between the cadet brigades at the bridges. Montclos's men were in position near the Breil racecourse, scene in times of peace of many a triumph of the *Cadre Noir.*

Michon was looking ahead now, on to Saumur itself. On the island Gérard de Buffévent and the 12th Brigade had already reported themselves ready, and Cadet Houbé was impatiently waiting to fire his 25 mm gun for the first time. In Saumur itself Périn de St-André and the 8th Brigade were grouped around another 25 mm gun near the town hall.

Moving east again, past the little house on the cliffs at the village of Petit-Puy, where Lieutenant de St-Germain, in overall command of the bridge brigades, had his command post, on to Hubert de la Lance's men at the railway viaduct, and finally at the eastern limit of his sector the iron bridge at Montsoreau. Here Lieutenant Jacques Trastour and the 9th Brigade were in position on the high ground above the bridge where rocks and caves provided good cover. One of his cadets, Bernard Gautier, with a couple of his comrades, was over the bridge on the north bank preparing a surprise for the Germans.

From his command post Colonel Michon could see all his bridges except those at Gennes, and he could see all the brigades that he had placed in position in the gaps along the river between the bridges. What he could not see, however, were the support squadrons that were in position about four kilometres back from the river and therefore in the countryside behind his own command post. Each group that was on the river defending the bridges or the gaps between them had a support group in the rear immediately behind it, ready to come to its aid depending on the circumstances of the battle.

Captain Foltz was at Milly-le-Meugon directly behind Gennes, ready to help Desplats on the island or Roimarmier at Thoureil.

Behind Commandant Hacquard's dragoons was Captain Marzolf's squadron, to which belonged Lieutenant Garnier's reconnaissance brigade, which was over the river in search of the enemy. Marzolf's men were at the village of Beaucheron waiting to be called to help Hacquard or Montclos.

On the other side of Saumur – out among the vineyards of Champigny, home of Saumur's celebrated *cru*, about four kilometres south of the river – was Captain de St-Blanquat's squadron, supporting Lieutenant de la Lance's brigade at the railway viaduct. Lieutenant Cadignan's group back at the abbey at Fontevrault were there to come to the aid of Lieutenant Trastour at the Montsoreau bridge and to keep contact with Colonel du Vigier's command to the east of the bridge towards Port-Boulet.

From Colonel Michon's viewpoint, however, the most important support group was the *Groupe Franc* of Captain de Neuchèze, experienced as a raiding group, mobile, armoured. This group he had in readiness behind his own command post; it was under his personal orders and he intended to use it as a mobile force to be rushed to any point of the sector at a moment's notice.

It was now evening and the light was fading. Lieutenant Poupon of the 6th Engineers arrived. When Colonel Michon gave the word, he would see to the blowing of the bridges. But even with the bridges blown, would they be able to stop the

Germans from getting over the river, Michon wondered. The river itself worried him. What little water there was shimmered in the moonlight. What he needed was a river in flood, not a river with exposed sandbanks that would help a determined invader get across. In normal times there would have been 50 metres of uninterrupted water between the banks, he reflected bitterly.

In the moonlight the houses of Saumur, like little boxes at the foot of the cliffs upon which Colonel Michon was standing, had all turned white, like the château that dominated everything. The silence that lay over the town, someone said later, was like the silence that precedes an earthquake or a tidal wave. It was the prelude to battle.

Suddenly the Colonel began to feel the pain of his old wounds of 1915, and he went back into the house. 'I shall have to stretch out on the mattress,' he told Commandant Lemoyne. 'Don't let me go to sleep and take over until I can get up again.'

At nine o'clock the telephone rang. Lemoyne took the call. Then he turned to Michon: 'It's the station-master at Saumur. He's just had a call from his colleague up the line. German columns, armoured and mechanized, have passed Château-du-Loir and Château-la-Vallière, advancing on Noyant. Then it will be Saumur.'

'Noyant!' repeated Michon, remembering Lieutenant Garnier's patrol that was across the river and now in danger of being cut off.

'Get Garnier back at once,' said Colonel Michon, getting up off his mattress. Then he gave the order that all had been waiting for: 'General alert to all units.'

4 Battle at the Bridges

The Germans reached the Loire at Saumur and came in sight of the Cavalry School, bathed in bright moonlight, a few minutes before midnight on Tuesday 18 June – cavalrymen with motorcycles and sidecars, followed by armoured cars. And they arrived where they had been expected, at the entrance to the bridge linking the north bank to Offard Island where Lieutenant Gérard de Buffévent and his twenty-four cadets of the 12th Brigade had been preparing their reception.

Now, for the first time, the cadets went into action, the sound of their automatic weapons contrasting stridently with the chiming of midnight from the ancient clocktowers of Saumur. The motorcyclists scattered before their fire. Then Cadet Houbé, manning the 25 mm gun, scored his first hit; by morning he had marked seven tanks and two armoured cars.

At twenty minutes past midnight a much more substantial noise was heard right along the sector. De Buffévent, acting on Colonel Michon's orders, had given the signal to the engineer officer, Lieutenant Poupon, who had then blown up the Pont Napoléon linking the island to the north bank. As the bridge went up, the island seemed to move under the force of the explosion. An hour later, like a delayed echo, came the sound of another explosion as the iron bridge at Montsoreau went up in the faces of the first German motorcyclists. At 3 a.m. the railway viaduct, so diligently mined by Sergeant Thelinge and his colleagues, also collapsed into the river.

The blowing of the bridge to Offard Island together with the fierce firing from de Buffévent's cadets had sent the advanced German cavalrymen hurrying for cover. But the Germans were not alone on the other side of the river. Soon after the blowing-up of the bridge, part of Lieutenant Garnier's reconnaissance brigade, called back by Colonel Michon earlier in the evening, arrived to find that their way back to the safety of Saumur had disappeared. And in the confusion of smoke and noise they were being fired on from the island by de Bufférent's cadets, their comrades. The reconnaissance party, led by an NCO, Marissen, pulled their motorcycles back into the shelter of the buildings.

The firing stopped and for a few moments there was silence. Then de Buffévent's men on the island heard an extraordinary sound coming to them over the river from the north bank, where they had seen the Germans arrive. It was the sound of a trumpet, and for all his worth the trumpeter was working his way as rapidly as possible through the French Army's repertoire of familiar and significant tunes – the General Salute, the Curfew, the Soup, the *Casquette du Père Bugeaud*, the General Assembly and then, finally, to the amazement of de Buffévent and his cadets, the Cease Fire. Was it a trick on the part of the Germans, they wondered, or had some French scout with a bugle in his haversack got himself stranded among the enemy on the other side of the river? They were not prepared to take any chances, and there was another volley of automatic rifle fire across the wrecked bridge.

At that moment Lieutenant Garnier himself arrived at de Buffévent's command post, having come from Saumur over the bridge to the island from the south bank, which was still intact. When he had received Colonel Michon's order to return a few hours earlier, he himself with part of the reconnaissance brigade had made for the Loire bridges at Gennes. He had ordered the rest of the group, which was being led by Marissen and patrolling further to the east, to make for Saumur direct and cross over the Pont Napoléon.

Reaching Gennes, Garnier had been told by Jacques Desplats that the Pont Napoléon had already been blown up. He then drove immediately to Saumur along the south bank of the river and, crossing over to the island, was able to explain to de Buffévent what had happened. The trumpeter was one of his own men who had desperately been trying to convey to de Buffévent's brigade that they were French, not German. At his headquarters de Buffévent had an old megaphone which he had used to call out to people living on the top storeys of buildings on the island when he had had to evacuate them. Garnier borrowed it and, creeping up to the edge of the broken bridge, began to shout for Marissen. The NCO appeared and Garnier told him to collect his men and ride away westward, avoiding the road along the north bank, bypassing Gennes, which he feared was already being threatened by the Germans. He should try to cross the river at Ponts de Cé over towards Angers and then make his way back to join Captain Marzolf's squadron, from which they had been originally detached and which was in reserve at Beaucheron, ready to go to the aid of Commandant Hacquard's group by the river.

But where were the Germans? After the first contact and the rapid firing which preceded the blowing-up of the bridges, the cadets, in their pent-up excitement, began to report their presence here, there and everywhere. Most of the sightings turned out to be false alarms – over-excited, they were seeing and hearing things: the crunch of armoured vehicles along the roads, rafts pushing off from out of the shadows. Lieutenant Rezel, commanding another brigade of Marzolf's squadron, was called suddenly to Breil upstream from Saumur; the Germans were crossing the river, it was said. He found nothing but shadows moving in the moonlight. Groups of cadets went dashing into the thickets and among the rose trees growing along the river banks; sometimes they fired off at what they thought was movement. But nothing happened. It was unnerving.

However, on the other side of the river the Germans were indeed moving about. Commandant Hacquard, from his command post at the Château de Chênehutte by the river on the way to Gennes from Saumur, had reported to Colonel Michon that he could see the German artillery assembling batteries of 77 mm and 105 mm guns in preparation, apparently, for a bombardment of Saumur. The crunching sound made by armoured vehicles, tanks and carriers on the asphalt was real enough. Then the Germans began to fire bright starshell in order to determine the nature of the resistance on the other bank, and in that sudden bright light the scattered brigades of Colonel Michon were able to see the considerable force that was assembling to do battle with them.

But would there be a battle? The Germans, it seemed, would

Cadet Guy Roland-Gosselin – his body was taken from the Loire by the monks of St Maur's Abbey and buried near their saint

Instructor Lieutenant Jacques Roimarmier's death is commemorated by a memorial stone at the side of the road to Angers where he fell

Lieutenant Alain Pitiot, a brilliant officer of the *Groupe Franc*, was killed in a suicidal tank attack at Aunis Farm

Cadet Raymond Deutz d'Arragon fought alongside Lieutenant Desplats, survived and, in due time, became a general

Instructor Lieutenant Gérard I
fort de Buffévent: 'My father
1914] was killed carrying t
ridingstock. So shall I be.'

like to have avoided it. During their approach to Saumur, their advance columns had already taken several prisoners, who included some of the cadets who had failed to get back from the reconnaissance patrol. According to the German account of these events, they had surprised and captured these young men, who, having failed to cross the river, had taken refuge in a farmhouse and fallen asleep. From them they learned for the first time that their adversary on the other side of the river was not the French Army but the cadets of the Cavalry School.

One of the German officers, Lieutenant von Engel, recorded: 'Two cadets made prisoner during the course of the first phase of the combat declared pathetically: ' "In Spain there was an Alcazar; in France there will be a Saumur." ' This was a reference to an incident in the Spanish Civil War in 1936 when 190 Spanish infantry cadets had bravely held out while besieged in their academy until rescued by troops of their own side.

The German cavalrymen had also intercepted another French patrol which had nothing to do with Colonel Michon's command but which, in trying to reach Saumur, had turned up on the north bank only to find the bridge had been destroyed. This was a detachment from the 201st Artillery depot. Seeing that the bridge was down, they turned away and took the road along the river going west to Les Rosiers. They had not gone far, however, when they were caught by the Germans. Their leader, Lieutenant Belisson, had gone on ahead to Gennes to see if the bridges were intact. Finding that they were, he then went back to fetch his men, ran into the Germans and was also made prisoner. Discovering that he spoke their language fluently, the Germans instructed him to act as interpreter to one of their senior officers who was about to parley with the French. Aware that armistice negotiations were going on, and wishing to avoid further fighting if that were possible, the Germans had decided to call on the French commander at Saumur to surrender the town in order to avoid its destruction by the artillery batteries which were in position and ready to go to work.

Just before dawn on Wednesday 19 June, an open touring car carrying the senior German officer with several of his staff, together with Lieutenant Belisson, drew up at the side of the road near the gap left by the wrecked Pont Napoléon. The German officer, with the French officer at his side, got out and began to walk towards the river, another German walking ahead with a small white flag in a frame. Suddenly all hell broke loose: on the island the 25 mm gun went into action accompanied by bursts of machine-gun fire. There was a tremendous explosion. When the smoke cleared, there was nothing left of the car but a pile of twisted metal. The Germans and the French officer lay dead in the roadway.

They had been killed under the white flag. How such a thing could have happened in such a place, at such a time, is a question that has never been satisfactorily answered, despite subsequent enquiries. Was it due to inexperience, to a misunderstanding? Had the cadets not seen the white flag and the French officer who was walking beside it or had they suspected a trick, knowing that by June 1940 there had been several incidents of treachery under the white flag? Or was it, as seems most probable, an accident produced by a long night of tension and nervous fingers on triggers? Whatever the explanation, it was an incident heavy with consequences for Saumur. There was now no question but that a battle would take place and that Saumur would not be spared the German shells. 'After this incident,' the German account narrates, 'the command of the 1st Cavalry Division decided on the bombardment of the town of Saumur by the 11/77 Regiment of Artillery.'

During 19 and 20 June 1940 some 2,000 shells hit Saumur, causing considerable damage to its ancient buildings. The Romanesque church of St-Nicholas, whose treasures had fortunately been removed to safety, received a direct hit, as did St-Pierre, whose clocktower tumbled in a heap behind the Cavalry School. The great château, only a short distance from Colonel Michon's command post at the Villa des Grandes Brises, was damaged – in particular the Horse Museum on an upper storey. But no German battery commander seems to have aimed a single shell at the elegant collection of 18th-century buildings that make the ensemble of the Cavalry School, although its exposed position in front of the river made it an easy target. The Hôtel Budan, overlooking the river next to the Cessart Bridge, and further into the town the Hôtel de Londres, both popular hostelries among British tourists of the 1930s, as they are today, were hit by the German shells.

Most serious for the Colonel defending Saumur was the destruction early on of the town's telephone exchange. With the telephone out of action and his radio equipment, which had previously been used for instructional purposes at the school and was very worn, barely able to function in the noisy atmosphere, he had to rely on dispatch riders on motorcycles to keep in contact with his brigades scattered over his wide sector.

To the Germans' great barrage of artillery fire Lieutenant Périn de St-André's cadets, from their positions in Saumur along the south bank of the river on either side of the Cessart Bridge, and from the town hall just behind, replied as best they could with their anti-tank guns, mortars and 25 mm gun. The instructor lieutenant was handling the gun himself, trying to follow the instructions coming from one of his cadets mounted on the roof of the municipal theatre who was directing him onto targets on the other side of the river. Other cadets were on the upper floor of the Hôtel Budan, trying to see where the enemy was firing from. The German artillery was well out of range, however, and there was nothing they could do to stop the shells coming their way.

There were lulls when the bombardment stopped. Soldiers and civilians would emerge from shelter to pick up the dead and wounded. Some of the civilian helpers were women. A couple of bakers, who throughout the shelling had not ceased their work, came out with fresh loaves and other supplies of food which they took from abandoned shops. These they handed to the young defenders in uniform at their battle stations and to the civilians sheltering in deep wine cellars. In one cellar alone, the enormous storage cavern of the *vigneron* Noël Tessier, some 2,000 people were sheltering in the dark, with little food and water. Parish priests moved among them, trying to give comfort and encouragement.

Offard Island, still linked to the rest of Saumur by the Cessart Bridge, could no longer be seen in the thick smoke that seemed to be everywhere. Gérard de Buffévent, who had lost none of his men in the exchange of fire with the Germans on the north bank, had, however, lost contact with the rest of the sector since the destruction of the telephone system. The Germans meanwhile were shelling the island like the rest of Saumur, but de Buffévent seemed quite impervious to danger as he ran from his command post in the grain merchant's premises to visit his cadets one by one at the points where he had placed them, preparing them with words of encouragement for a German landing on the island which he felt must come soon.

After a while de Buffévent was joined by Second Lieutenant d'Anglejan, who had been sent over from Saumur with a couple of armoured cars to help the 12th Brigade. In due course d'Anglejan left an account of these last hours on Offard Island. Gérard de Buffévent, he said, always had his curly pipe or a long cigarette-holder at his lips. Nor would he be separated from his cavalryman's riding stock, which had a special significance for him – his father had been carrying it when he had fallen in battle in 1914. 'My father was killed carrying this stock,' he told d'Anglejan. 'I shall be, too.' D'Anglejan found him in good spirits. He was not even put out when a very old woman, who had somehow been left behind when the other inhabitants of the island had been evacuated, walked into his command post and in a loud, high-pitched voice began to recite the prayers for the dead. She settled in a corner of the room and, when she was quiet, de Buffévent said to her: 'After the war, tell them my men were brave.'

A small projectile hit the room where de Buffévent and d'Anglejan were sitting and split the table between them but neither was hurt. However, they moved into an adjoining shed where the cadets in relays were being allowed a short time to sleep. Exhausted, they lay spreadeagled on the sacks of Monsieur Boret's grain that were piled up there.

During the morning, judging that he and his men were no longer serving any useful purpose by remaining on the island and that they would do better to reinforce Périn de St-André's brigade in Saumur itself, de Buffévent dispatched Cadet d'Elloy de Bonninghen to the south bank to go and tell Colonel Michon what he was proposing to do. He explained to his men that he would remain on the island with the crew of the 25 mm gun. He would be the last to leave the island, '… but before that we shall have destroyed the munitions and fought among the houses. You others will go to reinforce Lieutenant Périn's 8th Brigade and not worry about us even if the bridge is destroyed.'

Colonel Michon reacted strongly against the proposal brought to him by Cadet d'Elloy, who carried back written instructions to de Buffévent: 'I formally command you to hold the position till the death. Re-occupy it without any idea of withdrawal.' Gérard de Buffévent turned pale and his face contracted when he read the note, which he stuffed into his pocket. The reproach which he felt in his colonel's command, the misinterpretation perhaps of what he intended, as if he were trying to save his own skin, seemed to hurt him momentarily. As far as he was concerned, he would do exactly what his colonel had ordered; that, anyway, had always been his intention – to hold the position to the death.

As the afternoon of 19th June wore on, more and more of the island seemed to be burning: a grocery shop caught fire and, aided by the wind and some nearby petrol leaks, developed into an enormous blaze. It spread to a place where tar was being stored and came close to the gas factory. The fire was eventually brought under control when a single shot fired at the reservoir made it burn like a nightlight.

At six o'clock de Buffévent ordered d'Anglejan to return to his own unit in Saumur itself. It was only a matter of time before the bridge linking them to Saumur on the south bank, the Pont Cessart, would be destroyed, if not by the German shells then by the French engineers, and de Buffévent was concerned to get as much of their material, arms and ammunition – which would become increasingly precious as the battle was prolonged – off the island. The fact that by evening the Germans had still not attempted a landing on the island made him think that they were planning to cross the river elsewhere in order to get at Saumur. 'If the Germans get on the island,' he told d'Anglejan, 'we'll continue to hold the houses; blow up the bridge and don't worry about us.'

'I was almost weeping at having to leave him,' d'Anglejan wrote later to de Buffévent's mother. 'To console me he said, "If only you knew how much happier I am now than I was a couple of days ago when they nearly signed the armistice without our being beaten." '

As d'Anglejan and his companions were preparing to leave de Buffévent and the 12th Brigade on the island, up at the Villa des Grandes Brises the engineer officer Lieutenant Poupon was trying to convince Colonel Michon that 'because of the events on the island' he should not wait any longer but blow up Cessart

Bridge immediately. If the Germans suddenly appeared out of the smoke on the island, he argued, he might not have time to light the fuses under the bridge, and the enemy would be into the town. Michon agreed and at 7.30 that evening there was once again a tremendous explosion as the bridge went up, demolishing several nearby houses on the quay as it did so. Even those sheltering in the deep cellars felt the earth tremble violently. Second Lieutenant d'Anglejan and his companions had got across just in time. 'The defenders of the island,' wrote Colonel Michon in his report, 'remained in their positions.'

In the knowledge that there was no way forward and none back, Gérard de Buffévent and his cadets threw themselves once more into the combat with a kind of desperate joy. Like their comrades of Périn de St-André's 8th Brigade on the south bank of the river, the cadets on the island kept up a regular and consistently accurate fire on the German positions in the buildings on the north bank. The Germans could not – and never did – get over the island and into Saumur to the Cavalry School. On 3 July 1940 the German newspaper *Der Vormarsch*, describing what had happened at Saumur, wrote: 'The fire of our artillery never succeeded in paralysing the resistance of our adversary, to whose courage we render a tribute.'

During the night of 19 June Colonel von Edelsheim summoned his subordinate commanders to meet him and to reconsider their plan of action since, 'Saumur and the south bank of the Loire were occupied by an enemy whose strength was unknown.' They decided that they would have to get across the river up and down stream from Saumur and then take the town from behind. Von Edelsheim called in his engineer officer to talk about boats and rafts.

Over the river, high up on the cliffs at the Villa des Grandes Brises, Colonel Michon was also changing his plans. All the bridges on his sector were down except those at Gennes, where the Germans had only just made contact with Lieutenant Jacques Desplats's brigade, watching them arrive at Les Rosiers on the north bank from its position on the island. The Germans might make their major thrust at Gennes or might try elsewhere to cross the river. The defence of the sector would become increasingly complicated and require quick action as the situation changed.

Michon decided that he could no longer do this satisfactorily from his command post at the Villa des Grandes Brises. Deprived of his telephone and equipped with a radio upon which he could not rely, his dispatch riders were all-important to him but their journeys to and from the villa were becoming increasingly precarious. Since early afternoon the Germans had been shelling the heights with their 105 mm guns, whose position they could see from the roof of the villa. Lacking suitable guns of their own, Michon's men could do nothing about countering their deadly fire. Enemy aircraft flew overhead and seemed to be acting as observers for the artillery. The shells had ripped up the roads all round the villa, and Michon and his staff were feeling increasingly isolated.

Early in the evening they quit the villa in order to establish new headquarters some three kilometres to the west in the little Auberge de Marsoleau, an inn which was little more than a café near the airfield at Terrefort and close to where Michon had positioned the *Groupe Franc* of Captain de Neuchèze as his mobile reserve. Marsoleau, on a gentle wooded hillside well back from the river, was situated about halfway between Gennes and Montsoreau, the two ends of the sector that the Cavalry School was defending. From this new command post Michon felt he would be better able to use de Neuchèze's *Groupe Franc*. In fact, it had been his experience with this group earlier in the afternoon that had finally decided him to move his command post. From the Villa des Grandes Brises he had sent a radio message to de Neuchèze to make a rapid raid with his tanks and armoured cars over the Gennes bridges in order to attack from the rear the German positions at Saumur. The radio waves, however, were being dominated by the powerful radios of the Germans, and in the noisy atmosphere they had created de Neuchèze's radio operator never picked up the weak signal coming from Colonel Michon's inferior equipment. It was a lost opportunity that never returned, for late that afternoon the Germans began to arrive in force at the western end of the sector, at Les Rosiers and in front of Gennes, to join the battle that had already started in the east at Saumur and beyond at Montsoreau.

Throughout the afternoon of 19 June, while the bombardment was going on at Saumur, the cavalry cadets at Gennes with their Algerian comrades showed no sign of life. At 2.30 p.m. two German cars arrived at Les Rosiers, having come along the road from Saumur. Several German officers got out and began to ask the villagers if there were any French troops in the area. With their fieldglasses they examined the south bank at Gennes and the island. All was quiet. There seemed to be no one about. They got back into the car and returned towards Saumur.

At four o'clock a group of German motorcyclists arrived from Longué, and they too asked questions. Where were the French troops? Would the bridges be blown up? Then they too departed. Soon Jacques Desplats could see through his glasses that a considerable German force was moving towards them from Longué and that the motorcyclists had been its scouts sent on ahead to find out what was happening at the Gennes bridges. Desplats decided that the time had come to blow the suspension bridge linking his island to the north bank. He gave the sign to Lieutenant Falke of the 6th Engineers, and the job was done. At 6.30 Captain Foltz, who was waiting with his support squadron at Milly-le-Meugon a few kilometres directly south from Gennes, heard the tremendous explosion that not only cut through the iron ropes of the suspension bridge but shattered the windows of nearby houses and sent forty kilos of iron flying through the roof of the Hôtel de la Loire – to the consternation of the Barrau sisters, two maiden ladies who were its owners.

Foltz decided to go himself to find out what was going on. At Gennes he climbed up into the tower of the eleventh-century church of St-Eusèbe with its elegant fifteenth-century steeple and found one of Desplats's cadets who had been posted there as an observer. The German scouts had come and gone. There seemed to be no sign of movement from the enemy. He reported back to Colonel Michon, who noted in his record: 'Sector calm.' It was, however, the lull before the storm, for it was at Gennes, in a short while, that the Germans would launch their first major assault against Colonel Michon's forces. Unknown to Captain Foltz, they were already installing their artillery in the orchards round Longué in preparation for the attack. Foltz, having inspected Desplats's positions on the island, returned to his men at Milly-le-Meugon.

The parish priest at Milly-le-Meugon was the Abbé Souillot. In the early hours of Wednesday 19 June, Instructor Lieutenant

Jean-Jacques Bonnin, commanding the 24th Brigade in Captain Foltz's squadron, went to the priest's house and got him out of bed. In the distance, from Saumur, they could hear the guns firing.

'We have been put on alert, *monsieur le curé*,' Bonnin told Abbé Souillot. 'At any moment we may be called by our comrades at Gennes to join the combat there. It will be hard. At all cost we shall have to hold out. You've seen our arms. We've no illusions. Many of us will not survive. Will you come to the church? I would like to be able to let the men in their various encampments know that a priest is at their disposal.'

Abbé Souillot complied immediately. The church remained open throughout the night, and it was never empty. Some eighty cadets and their instructors, almost the entire force encamped at Milly-le-Meugon, came to the church, in small groups, in full uniform, booted, helmeted, armed, ready at a moment's notice to go to battle. Outside in the square the engines of their motorcycles had been left running. Lieutenant Bonnin and Cadet Thibault assisted the priest throughout the night as, with the sound of gunfire in their ears, he gave Holy Communion. After the war, writing of that night, Abbé Souillot maintained that in June 1940 the cavalry cadets of Saumur had in modern form repeated what their ancestors had done at the time of the Crusades or the knights in the Middle Ages, who, leaving their horses outside, ready and waiting, had knelt at the Communion table before departing for battle. Today a stained glass window in the church at Milly-le-Meugon, showing the Cadets of Saumur at prayer there on the night of 19 June 1940, on the eve of battle, is a poignant reminder of the events of those days. And for Lieutenant Jean-Jacques Bonnin, whose faith and piety had inspired the armed vigil in the church, it was also to be a memorial.

By eight o'clock on the evening of 19 June another little church and another priest had become the centre of attention at the western end of Colonel Michon's sector. Abbé Gaultier was just about to close his church on the little square at Les Rosiers on the north bank of the river facing Gennes, after watching the arrival of some fifty German troop-carriers packed with assault troops, when he was approached by three German officers. The tall, blonde, hatless one asked him to take them up to the top of the clocktower. The Abbé told them that the tower was locked and that the Mayor had the key. They then told him to take them to the Mayor. Monsieur Bougieau produced the key and went along with the others back to the church. The Mayor and the priest waited at the foot of the stairs while the German officers and some of their men climbed up into the tower. They were looking for a place to set up their radio and aerial.

At that moment the clock in the tower began to strike nine o'clock, and before it had ceased to strike, the tower was hit by a sharp burst of machine-gun fire coming from the island that lay between Les Rosiers and Gennes. Desplats's cadets, hidden in the bushes with their weapons, had gone into action. They pitted the tower, but the clock remained unharmed and continued to chime. After a short pause, however, it began to chime nine times once again. This time Desplats's 25 mm gun from its position in Gennes itself went into action. The shell hit the tower but did not explode. The clock went on chiming.

The Germans were convinced by this time that they were the victims of a trick, that somehow, through the chiming of the clock (they were apparently unfamiliar with repeater clocks), the priest was passing signals to the defending force on the island. With the butts of their rifles the Germans smashed the mechanism of the clock and then hurried down the stairs, where they seized the priest and Mayor as hostages. 'You'll both be shot,' the big blonde German, furious at the turn of events, told them. Strongly denying that they had had anything to do with the attack on the tower, they were nevertheless marched out under guard into the square of Les Rosiers, where they were to spend the next two days in great discomfort expecting from one minute to the next to be shot.

While the Mayor of Les Rosiers and the priest stood helplessly in the square, all round them the Germans were launching a furious attack on the island and on Gennes itself. German machine-guns were installed in the upper windows of houses along the river on the north side and on the first floor of the Hôtel des Ducs d'Anjou, and kept up a persistent fire towards the island. At the same time shells from their artillery batteries in the orchards round Longué, several kilometres behind them, were causing havoc in Gennes, setting its houses on fire, and on the island, where whole trees were ripped out of the ground, splitting their trunks like matchsticks. The precious fifteenth-century steeple of St-Eusèbe, the pride and joy of Abbé Moissinac, was hit – its tumbling masonry injured several people in the streets below. The tower itself became untenable as an observation post for the cadet who had been trying to direct the fire of Desplats's 25 mm gun, which had been placed under cover of the wall surrounding the church grounds.

Desplats realized that the tremendous barrage the Germans had mounted could only mean that they were preparing to get men in boats and rafts onto the island and then into Gennes itself. The island was about two kilometres long, and at its widest about 200 metres. His cadets and the Algerian riflemen were well hidden in the trees and bushes but these made it difficult for them to see what the Germans were doing. Groups of cadets with their machine-guns were moved hurriedly from one part of the island to another. Jean-Louis Dunand, with his eighteen-year-old comrade Guy Roland-Gosselin, hurriedly reassembled their machine-guns on the western tip of the island in order to prevent a landing by German troops who, embarking in rafts upstream and coming down with the strong current, might have taken them from behind. To the eastern end of the island, in bright moonlight across open ground, ran Raymond Deutz d'Arragon and the two cadets he had mentioned in his last letter to his parents, de Farcy, who was to become a Jesuit priest and the seventeen-year-old Baron Bertrand de Bellaing, the latter carrying the machine-gun on his broad, athletic shoulders.

Desplats's problem was to try to anticipate where the German assault troops would land. The young Germans, like their young French adversaries, seemed to be buoyed up and excited by the conditions of the battle, impervious to its dangers, singing loudly as they propelled their pneumatic rafts across the water. Again and again the sharp fire from the cadets drove them back, capsizing their canoes, pitching them into the water. Both sides were losing men – Cadet Joseph Lemaître fell with six bullets in his body and would soon have to be evacuated. Jacques Desplats, their leader, was tireless, moving from one group to the next, trying to anticipate the next assault across the river. Some of the Germans pitched into the water, refused to give up and swam on towards the island with their weapons. Some got a foothold on a sandbank to the east of the island but were driven off by Dunand and Roland-Gosselin, assisted by Desplats himself and a sudden intervention from Lieutenant Roimarmier and his Service Corps cadets, who came running in from east of Gennes when they saw what was happening. One cadet even managed to puncture a German canoe with a bayonet. Half an hour before midnight the Germans broke off the action, and all was quiet on the front.

Despite the bombardment, the telephone exchange at Gennes was still functioning, though it would not be for very much longer. Madame Rocher, Mademoiselle Lauzie and Monsieur Denouault had at no time abandoned their posts, and they were able to get Jacques Desplats on the line to Captain Foltz.

'Everything is going well,' Desplats reported. 'The enemy has not got over the Loire. Morale is excellent.'

The word was passed on, first to Colonel Michon and from him to General Pichon at Azay-le-Rideau.

'At the end of the day,' Colonel Michon reported, 'all our positions are being held in their entirety, all attempts to cross have been pushed back by our automatic weapons and our mortars. Those brigades that have been engaged have magnificently got on top of a relentless and powerfully armed enemy.'

These were proud words but they were premature. The silence over the river at midnight on 19 June did not mean that the battle was over. It was true that the Germans had been surprised by the spirited defence offered them on the river, and they seemed to be uncertain of the strength of the French forces defending this stretch of the Loire. Those in charge of the advance guard even wondered, according to the German account, if they ought not to await the arrival at the river of the full division before relaunching the battle.

At midnight the engineer officer at Gennes blew up the last bridge on the sector, the suspension bridge linking the island with Gennes on the south bank. Fearing that when the bombardment started again it might interfere with his charges, he acted on his own initiative and did not consult Desplats, who, to his chagrin, found himself cut off on the island from those of his cadets whom he had posted in Gennes to man his 25 mm guns. Like his friend Gérard de Buffévent on Offard Island upstream at Saumur, he was now effectively isolated, for the telephone connection had also been broken.

Captain Foltz at Milly-le-Meugon decided to send Albert de Galbert with the 29th Brigade, riding motorcycles, together with an armoured car, to find out what was happening at Gennes. With the bridge down, de Galbert slipped across to the island in a boat. He found Jacques Desplats in good heart.

'My orders are to resist at all cost,' he told de Galbert. 'We'll resist.'

'He told me he had repulsed the first attack,' de Galbert wrote later. 'He had not a word of complaint, not even of being tired. I thought that if I had been in his place I would have been tempted to complain. No, he just spoke to me of his men, of their food, of their morale, which was very good. What a leader! What soldiers!'

Both these young officers had happier memories of Gennes, of dinners at the excellent hotel run by the Barrau sisters. Desplats and his wife, together with other young married instructors, the Périn de St-Andrés, the Trastours and the Puzenets, would travel over together from Saumur for an agreeable evening at the Barraus' table. That had been only a matter of weeks ago; now it was like an eternity away in time.

Jacques Desplats had the reputation among his cadets of being distant and reserved – Bernard de Bellaing remembered him as being a '*grand seigneur*'. All this seemed to change in the intimacy of their island existence, whose dangers brought a new relationship between instructor and pupils; all had become comrades-in-arms. 'Always up during the firing, giving orders with that calm that we knew, the whole night he was organizing our defence, assigning us our posts, superintending the evacuation of the wounded,' Cadet de Farcy recorded. 'In the middle of the night the first German attempt at a landing, and then a second was repulsed.'

After the Germans had broken off the attack, Desplats's concern was with his casualties. De Galbert's visit provided the opportunity to evacuate them. Cadet Norbert Bontoux, who had been doing his best to get Desplats's worn-out radio equipment to work, was detailed to help get the wounded over the river to Gennes. In his boat he took his suffering comrade Joseph

Lemaître, who constantly asked for water to quench his terrible thirst, and he took the wounded NCO Ritter, who had been in charge of the Algerian riflemen. De Galbert then followed, having managed to embark the body of a dead rifleman, Mohammed Dachir, into his boat. The cadets struggled with the dead weight of the giant Algerian. De Galbert quoted Scripture at them: 'He who provides a sepulchre for the dead will himself be given one when his turn comes.' He added: 'It's tough, anyway, to have to fight alongside a corpse.' Then they watched him go, pulling strongly on the oars. Reaching Gennes, de Galbert had the Algerian buried in the garden of Monsieur Bonnifet's house near the river.

On the island, waiting for the battle to begin again, the cadets tried to clean their rifles, which had become clogged with grit and sand. Desplats told them to dismantle them as he had shown them in class, clean them and then re-assemble them. There was no oil to clean them with. Among their paltry stores someone found some olive oil that was used for cooking. They made do with that. Some of the cadets were showing signs of exhaustion. To one of them who was quenching his thirst at a well by the little farmhouse which Desplats was using as his command post, his instructor said: 'Don't worry, everything's all right. We've just got to hold on and stay calm.' And with that Desplats set off yet again to visit his men, his adoring Airedale, Nelson, always at his side. Seemingly unaffected by the noise of gunfire, the dog would often bound ahead of its master, sniffing out the cadets hiding in the bushes as if it were a game.

In the early hours of Thursday 20 June, Desplats, watching Les Rosiers through his glasses, saw the arrival of German reinforcements, great six-wheeled vehicles from which an interminable number of *Feldgrauen* seemed to be disembarking. These were the German infantry that had been attached to the Cavalry Division. At the same time the German engineers were assembling an armada of unorthodox floats, rafts made from doors taken from houses at Les Rosiers, and enormous casks converted to little boats. From the square at Les Rosiers the mayor and the priest were taken before a senior German officer and warned that, if any more clock signals were sent off or any attempt was made by the people of Les Rosiers to help the defence on the other side of the river and on the island, it would be so much the worse for them. In any case they would be detained until the battle was over.

The Germans had scheduled their attack for five o'clock in the morning. Just before dawn their artillery, the 77 mm, 105 mm and 150 mm guns at Longué, began their usual overture, this time with all the stops out. Shells were bursting in profusion over Gennes and the island. And on the dot of five o'clock the Germans launched their massive attack across the river, not only onto the island but directly towards the south bank at Gennes. Desplats's men tried desperately to stop the landings on the island, while on the river bank at Gennes de Galbert's cadets scored numerous hits on the waterborne Germans. But the French were few and the Germans were many and could not be stopped.

On the island the battle was soon over, the Germans taking their toll of Desplats's little brigade. Jean-Louis Dunand, though wounded, went on firing until killed by a shell. His comrade Guy Roland-Gosselin was hit in the right hand and, trying to escape the Germans advancing on him, dived into the river and tried to swim to safety but was hit almost immediately. His body floated down river and was later taken from the water by the monks of the Abbey of St-Maur who buried him in the little cemetery near the tomb of their saint. It was an honourable resting-place for the eighteen-year-old cadet, who was the nephew of the Bishop of Versailles.

Cadet Brasseur, pipe in mouth, was hurling a grenade when he was killed.

Braillard, an NCO who was twice the age of the cadets, was killed in the same way. 'One will die,' he used to say before the battle, 'but France will be saved.'

And their leader, Jacques Desplats himself, was hit while making a desperate one-man effort to stop a German landing. He crawled under a willow tree and was putting a bandage on his leg when shells burst all round him, and he never moved again.

With their instructor dead and several of their colleagues, and when their ammunition ran out, what was left of the 11th Brigade could offer no more resistance. Two of the cadets succeeded in swimming back to Gennes; the others threw their weapons in the river, lit a cigarette and waited defiantly with their hands in their pockets. Later they accompanied their German captors on a tour of the island in search of the dead and wounded. Thus in the middle of the morning they found the body of Jacques Desplats. The dog Nelson, which had been hurt, lay shivering and whining next to its master. One of the cadets asked the German cavalry captain if he might be allowed to put the poor animal out of its misery. 'I myself will do it,' the German captain said, 'in memory of your leader', and with a revolver shot he dispatched Nelson to join his master.

When the Germans had possession of the island, with starshell they signalled as much to their artillery well back behind them. From Gennes, however, on the south bank, they were still meeting fierce resistance. Below the grounds of the battered church of St-Eusèbe a tremendous battle was going on. Captain Foltz, on Colonel Michon's instructions, had moved all his men into Gennes during the night. De Galbert and his 27th Brigade had been joined at the river by the 24th Brigade commanded by Jean-Jacques Bonnin and two others commanded by Lieutenant le Comte de Parcevaux and Lieutenant Alex Pasquet. Jacques de Parcevaux was in proud possession of three machine-gun carriers, ancient Renaults from the First World War, whose overheating engines threatened to boil over as he patrolled up and down the river.

With their meagre resources these four brigades put up such a strong resistance that the Germans were unable to get off the island and into Gennes. They decided, therefore, to move downstream towards Angers to the part of the river that Lieutenant Roimarmier and his company of Service Corps cadets were trying to cover with insufficient men and arms. Here the Germans found a large gap and began to make for it in force.

Roimarmier, from his command post at the Villa Montebello just below the road from Gennes to Angers, soon saw what the Germans were up to; a champion rifleshot, he picked them off one by one as they came out of the trees, a couple of his cadets feeding him with cartridges. But there were too many of them. He grabbed an automatic weapon and at the same time ordered his cadets to withdraw to safety along the road before they were surrounded. With the machine-gun he tried to hold off the German advance until his men had got away. As the Germans came on, he moved backwards up the stone steps of the villa leading to the road, firing his machine-gun as he went. A shell burst beside him, taking his left arm at the shoulder, and almost immediately he was hit again in the head. When, after the battle, they found his body, the fingers of his right hand still gripped the trigger of his gun. The shelling had also killed his valued NCO Gaillouste.

Without their leader, the Service Corps brigades tried to regroup in order to re-enter the battle but it was already too late, for the Germans now had a bridgehead on the south bank of the Loire from which they could move against Gennes.

It was only after the battle that they discovered what Roimarmier and his cadets had had to put up with. In their remote position to the west of Gennes, which was really the limit of Michon's sector, they had not been able to get food supplies for nearly three days. They were starving. Among Roimarmier's papers were copies of the messages he had sent off. 'I have the honour to inform you,' he told Colonel Michon, 'that the supplies which were supposed to reach me on the evening of 18 June did not arrive. The resources of the area are nil. Half my men have been without food for twenty-four hours. The supplies which were supposed to come on the morning of the 18th arrived at 1400 hours and were naturally insufficient.' As a postscript he added a pathetic plea: 'I am asking for at least a few bits of bread.' The following evening, 19 June, he wrote again: 'I advise you that at 20.30 hours no supplies have reached me.' Apart from appealing for food, he had also asked for ammunition.

Roimarmier's death at the age of thirty-one, commemorated by a memorial stone at the side of the road to Angers where he fell, ended another chapter in the long military history of his family. His great-grandfather had been one of Napoleon's carabineers at Waterloo; his grandfather had been wounded twice in the Crimea, won the Military Medal at Inkerman and been promoted at Sebastopol. In 1926, when he died in his ninety-ninth year – the doyen of holders of the Military Medal, his grandson Jean-Pierre, at seventeen, was already preparing for his entry to the Cavalry School at Saumur which had been a familiar landmark all his life and in whose defence, in the end, he was to perish.

Having established their bridgehead on the south bank of the Loire, the Germans were now preparing to move eastward again, towards Gennes and Saumur itself, and Captain Foltz, still holding Gennes, had to take steps immediately to try to stop them. Colonel Michon, back at his command post at the Auberge de Marsoleau, was doing his best to get reinforcements to him.

What the Commandant of the Cavalry School lacked most of all in his efforts to stop the Germans was artillery; he had nothing with which to reply to the incessant bombardment coming from the German guns that remained out of range of his own weapons. General Pichon knew this and the previous evening had sent an order to Captain Chanson commanding a detachment of artillery at Chinon to move three 75 mm guns to Colonel Michon as rapidly as possible. Michon was informed that they were on their way. General Pichon sent another order to Chinon, this time to a Captain Bleuze, who had three infantry companies. They, too, were ordered to go to Colonel Michon without delay. The men of these companies, like those in Colonel Michon's brigades, were mostly teenage boys; they, too, were pupil officers, but of the Infantry, and had been brought over from the infantry school at St-Maixent, some 140 kilometres to the south of the Loire.

On the evening of 18 June the infantry cadets had been told that their courses had been suspended at St-Maixent and that they would be standing by to move up to the combat zone on the Loire. The next day the St-Maixent battalion travelled to Chinon, where it was divided into two parts. One was to help defend the bridge at Port-Boulet, where the French engineers for once had failed in their task – their explosion had only damaged the bridge, which could still be crossed by light vehicles. The other contingent, under Captain Bleuze's command, was dispatched in the middle of the night to Colonel Michon, who was waiting to rush them to Captain Foltz's aid at Gennes.

'We slept in the trucks as they went along,' Cadet Pierre Gentil recorded. 'Some of the Germans had got across the Loire being defended by the Cavalry School and we had to stop their advance. At dawn we got down from our vehicles in the shelter of a wood. At times we could hear the guns firing. Then another order came and we got back into the trucks. We went on for a while, then stopped again and disembarked. Another counter-order.'

What was happening was that during Thursday 20 June the fortunes of battle were changing so quickly on Colonel Michon's sector of the Loire that he was having to change his orders in order to meet them. In the event, the infantry cadets from St-Maixent on their way to help Captain Foltz were turned back before they could get to Gennes, for while they were on the road the Germans had managed to get another bridgehead on the south bank, this time to the east of Gennes and closer to Saumur, which was in danger of being taken from the rear. Michon and his chief-of-staff, Lemoyne, were desperately trying to plug holes in the defence and had engaged all their reserves. Foltz never received any extra men. Nor did the three 75 mm guns ever do anything for the beleaguered cadet brigades. Sent at a moment's notice from one place to the next, they never fired a single shot; they probably could not have done so in any case, since later they were discovered to have a faulty mechanism.

No infantrymen turned up at Foltz's command post at Gennes. In their place came Captain Choppin, one of Colonel Michon's liaison officers. He brought orders for Captain Foltz to make a counter-attack in order to retake the lost positions which now formed the German bridgehead on the south bank of the river where Roimarmier's company had been. Two tanks and a platoon from Captain de Neuchèze's *Groupe Franc* were on their way to help Foltz with his counter-attack. Foltz selected Albert de Galbert for the seemingly impossible task of dislodging the Germans. It was 1.30 p.m.

At that very moment – 1.30 on the afternoon of Thursday 20 June 1940, the Commander-in-Chief, General Weygand, together with Marshal Pétain and the rest of the Government at Bordeaux, received at last, by radio, the German Government's instructions for the French armistice delegation. The French envoys were to present themselves on the Loire bridge near Tours at five o'clock that afternoon. Firing would be suspended in the area of the Tours–Poitiers road and on the river, to allow the French peace convoy to cross safely into the German lines.

The wait seemed interminable to General Weygand, who as

Defence Minister had joined his Cabinet colleagues in asking the Germans for an armistice but as Commander-in-Chief had instructed his soldiers to fight on – for the honour of the Army and for no other reason, since the war was lost. 'How many days should we have to wait,' he was to write, 'and meanwhile what would happen to our military situation?'

The first response from Hitler to the French approach made through the Spanish Government on 17 June had come on the morning of 19 June, when he asked for the names of the French armistice delegation. The Foreign Minister Baudouin then asked Weygand if he himself would lead the delegation. However, for Weygand, who in 1918 as Marshal Foch's chief-of-staff had actually read out France's peace terms for the defeated Germans in the railway carriage at Réthondes, such a suggestion was barely tactful. He replied that he was ready for any personal sacrifice but recalled that in 1918 the Germans had not sent their Commander-in-Chief or any top-ranking general to the armistice table, so he did not feel his presence was required. He nominated General Huntziger to lead the delegation to treat with the Germans. This was also ironic, since Huntziger was the officer who would have taken Weygand's place as Commander-in-Chief if Reynaud had followed de Gaulle's advice and removed Weygand. He was to have Weygand's job, after all, but it was not the one he had had in mind. For a man of Huntziger's dynamic and combative temperament, to have to lead a delegation suing for peace was a cruel destiny. The interview with Weygand was painful. 'It went to my heart,' Weygand recorded.

At 5 a.m. on 20 June, the German cavalry, supported by infantry, downstream from Tours at Gennes, were launching their attack against the little island being defended by Jacques Desplats and his cadets. At the same time, the French Commander-in-Chief received from the German Government in Berlin approval for the peace delegation. At 1.30 p.m., when Captain Foltz was ordered to make an impossible counter-attack at Gennes, General Weygand received the German instruction for Huntziger's convoy of cars to cross the Loire at Tours. Half an hour later the ten cars carrying the armistice envoys were on the road, General Huntziger having received his final instructions from Pétain, Weygand and Baudouin.

Captain Foltz had received his orders from Colonel Michon: re-occupy the lost positions of the morning. Captain Choppin had barely left him to return to his colonel when Albert de Galbert came into the command post and heard the news.

De Galbert was utterly fearless; his energy and calm were infectious, and under his leadership nothing seemed impossible to the cadets who were in his charge. Under bombardment or in the midst of rifle fire, he would give the impression of being out on some sort of ramble. The future General de Galbert, Governor of Les Invalides, was born to be a soldier. He had been a baby in arms when his father, after serving on Joffre's staff, had been killed leading his battalion of Alpine troops into action. Like Jean-Pierre Roimarmier, he had been educated at the old Prytanée military school at La Flèche before becoming a cavalry cadet and top of his promotion at Saumur.

'I wondered if I would ever see you again,' Foltz said as de Galbert, after a particularly difficult session with the Germans on the river, looked into the command post.

'Why was that?' asked de Galbert with a large grin.

Foltz gave him an affectionate slap on the back and then once more looked serious. 'We've orders to make a counter-attack,' he said. 'We've got to get back our positions of this morning.' He told de Galbert about the tanks coming from de Neuchèze.

'Right,' said de Galbert, who was in high spirits. 'With reinforcements like that, we can do it.' Then, turning to the cadet who was waiting behind him, he said briskly, '*En avant* – forward.'

'*Mon lieutenant*, you are sending me to my death,' the cadet said.

'I do you that honour, sir,' was his instructor's cheerful reply. And with that they were gone once more into the battle.

With the support of the tanks, de Galbert launched himself furiously against the German bridgehead on the south bank, drove the enemy back and re-occupied their positions. At 3 p.m. Foltz was able to inform Colonel Michon: 'We have pushed back the Germans; all the left bank of the Loire in the Gennes sector is in our hands.'

De Galbert's spirited action was, however, but an isolated incident, a brief setback for the Germans who everywhere else were pushing through on Colonel Michon's sector. Casualties among the French brigades were becoming increasingly heavy. From a group of twelve men from Lieutenant Bonnin's brigade who had gone forward to attack the German positions, moving on their stomachs or in sudden quick bounds, only five had come back. Among the cadets, however, there was no slackening of morale. In the midst of battle some of them could even sustain a sense of humour. Such was Cadet Gillet, who came from Burgundy and who, mounting his musket on an empty case of a famous Beaune *crû*, announced to his comrades: 'At least I shall have the satisfaction of imagining myself dying at home.'

Jacques de Frenne de Tiège was a keen boy scout. Small, thin, with a gentle face and bright, intelligent eyes, he was one of de Galbert's most popular cadets. During the course, so suddenly interrupted, he had been an outstanding pupil, and de Galbert had appointed him his deputy. As fearless as his leader, he went forward with a machine-gun, firing on a German 37 mm which was causing considerable damage in Gennes. Having silenced it, he began to run back to where he had left his motorcycle on the ground; his helmet was blown off but he ran on bareheaded until a burst of rifle fire brought him down for ever.

Cadet Felix Pineau had been killed running to the aid of a wounded comrade. Pierre Bugain, who had written to his parents at Amiens a moving account of the armed vigil in the church at Milly-le-Meugon, steadfastly held the position allotted to him despite the intensity of the German shelling and remained there firing his automatic rifle until mortally wounded. He died at the dressing station at Doué la Fontaine. At his side, after two hours of suffering, died Didier Flandin. He, too, the previous day had written to his parents: 'The war so far has spared me. I am almost ashamed.' And to his brother: 'Just a word or two in case God should call me … I have accepted my task gladly. I am sure our country will live….' Didier Flandin had been manning Desplats's 25 mm gun near St-Eusèbe church and had been on his way to get ammunition when caught in shellfire.

The death of Lieutenant Jean-Jacques Bonnin, the young instructor who had gone in the night to the Abbé Souillot to ask him to come to the church at Milly-le-Meugon, was another matter. In his official report Colonel Michon stated: 'Lieutenant

Bonnin during the defence of Gennes was mortally wounded by an enemy spy.'

The circumstances were mysterious. Cadet Jean Labuzan had been talking to Bonnin, who, lying on his stomach, was trying to return the enemy's fire coming across from the island. To the cadet their position seemed hopeless.

'*Mon lieutenant*,' he was saying, 'there are only five of us and we're overwhelmed. We're struggling against machine-guns. What do you think we should do now?'

'Hold on,' Bonnin said firmly. 'Hold on to the end, that was the order, you know that.'

'But we'll be taken prisoner. If we pull back now, we'll still be able to do some good work and will be able to resist longer,' the cadet insisted.

'My orders were to stay here with you in this very place,' Bonnin said, 'to the death.'

'All right,' Labuzan countered. 'One is ready to die but not to die for nothing.'

'No one dies for nothing,' Bonnin said quietly, according to Labuzan later. 'We shall all die for France.'

At that moment two civilians appeared among the houses; each man was dressed in a smock and carried what looked like a shopping bag on his arm. Bonnin went over and spoke to them, telling them to take cover as they were in danger of being hit. The younger of the two men said they were out trying to find bread. Bonnin half turned and was about to move back between the houses when the young man suddenly produced a weapon from under the bag on his arm and shot him in the back of the neck. Labuzan reacted immediately, bringing down the assailant with his own gun, but then had to cope with the other man, the elder of the two. He and Labuzan seemed to fire simultaneously. Both fell. Labuzan was wounded, the civilian was dead.

Almost at once, rescuers picked up Bonnin and Labuzan and got them to the field ambulance at Doué la Fontaine. The medical officer began to attend to Bonnin, who insisted that he should first treat the wounded cadets, including Labuzan. He asked the nursing nun to bring him paper and pencil and painfully began to write a report in which he recommended for Labuzan the immediate award of the Military Medal, but he was unable to finish it. He died in the early hours of Friday 21 June. Cadet Labuzan survived and later recounted to Abbé Souillot what had happened.

It transpired eventually that the two civilians had been lodging at Gennes for several days, passing themselves off as Belgian refugees. When in due course the Germans entered Gennes, their attention was drawn by a French civilian to the two bodies lying in the street. Identity discs, giving name and rank, were found under their clothing. A German officer quickly assembled a squad which saluted smartly as the bodies were carried away. All that the people of Gennes were able to discover later was that the elder of the two dead was a German officer of some importance. That there were Germans disguised as refugees operating on the south bank of the Loire well before the German Cavalry Division began its attack on Saumur was to become clearer when the battle developed at the other end of Colonel Michon's sector, around the wrecked iron bridge at Montsoreau on that decisive Thursday 20 June.

Meanwhile, early that same morning Lieutenant Gérard de Buffévent, marooned with his handful of cadets among the smoking ruins on Offard Island in front of Saumur, was growing increasingly convinced that the Germans had abandoned the idea of taking Saumur in a frontal attack across the island. He believed they had already gone east towards Montsoreau Bridge. If this were so, his mind was telling him, then what he should do was to get himself off the island and onto the north bank and try to take the Germans from behind with a surprise attack. Through his glasses he could make out a German mortar some way off, upstream towards Montsoreau, which was firing on his comrades across the river on the south bank; to silence the mortar would be his first objective.

De Buffévent had correctly anticipated German intentions. The mortar he could see was one of those that would provide the bombardment to cover the German assault across the river. The Germans had assembled a small armada of boats, canoes, pneumatic rafts, at Villebernier, and these they would launch across the river to the little beach below the cliffs on which stood the village of Petit-Puy and the house where Lieutenant St-Germain had his command post, and further east Dampierre, where Hubert de la Lance was entrenched near the ruined railway viaduct. Abandoning a frontal attack on Saumur, they were going to attempt a crossing east of the town. The question of where they should cross the river had already caused dissent among the Germans, according to their own account. The senior engineer attached to the Cavalry Division was insisting that his boats should all cross together to the west of Saumur, towards Gennes. Colonel von Edelsheim, however, maintained that they should cross both upstream and downstream from Saumur. The engineer felt that the sandbanks to the east of Saumur would slow up the boats, and in the end he declined to accept responsibility. Von Edelsheim went ahead. Throughout the early hours of Thursday 20 June the Germans, maintaining an incredible silence as they worked, prepared for the crossing of the Loire scheduled for 6.30 in the morning.

It was the silence on the river that tempted Gérard de Buffévent to go and see what was happening on the north bank – and this despite his enormous fatigue. Still suffering the effects of a recent illness, it was only the determination of an iron will that kept him going. He had had no rest during the night. At one point Cadet Chresteil, hearing a bump outside the command post, went out to investigate and found de Buffévent sprawled out on the ground.

'It's nothing,' he said. 'Just giddiness.' He got to his feet again. 'Haven't you noticed anything?' he asked the cadet, then, motioning him to follow, went towards the river. 'The Germans have gone off towards the viaduct,' he said. 'They want to outflank Saumur, but that's their business. I'm sure there's no one here in front of us; those tanks are probably not even guarded, perhaps a man or two with the mortars.' He surveyed the north bank through his glasses. 'I'm going to have a look,' he told Chresteil. 'You stay here with the others. If I don't get back, you will have to take over.'

They went back to the command post and de Buffévent called for a volunteer to accompany him. Everyone volunteered and he chose Cadet Raveton. Together they pushed off in a little boat to the north bank. Not a single shot from the Germans. No sound.

'You see,' de Buffévent said. 'I was right. Not even a cat.'

They returned to the island, and once more de Buffévent called for volunteers, this time for a patrol in depth. Once more de Buffévent and Raveton, joined by Cadet Lederlin, crossed over in the boat. Fifteen minutes later a second boat, carrying Cadets Douzou, de Martignac and Thevin, followed. All were to meet at a little farmhouse that de Buffévent had pointed out to them on the north bank, some way back from the river to the east of the island. Leaving Raveton there to wait for the others, de Buffévent and Lederlin set off on a reconnaissance.

Tremendously tall, his long cigarette-holder in his mouth, his revolver in his hand, de Buffévent bounded forward on his long, ungainly legs. Cadet Lederlin, grasping his automatic rifle, did his best to follow. They came up onto the main road from Angers to Tours, the Nationale 152, but had not gone far when round the corner came a German motorcyclist, who, seeing them, tried to turn, skidded on the road and fell. 'Shoot,' shouted de Buffévent at Lederlin but the cadet's weapon jammed and the German ran off. De Buffévent, furious, ordered Lederlin back to the farmhouse to get a weapon that functioned, and, setting the motorcycle alight, went in search of the German with his revolver, fearing the motorcyclist would alert his comrades. Eventually the cadets at the farmhouse saw de Buffévent coming back; he had lost his helmet and was breathless from the chase, which had been fruitless. He collapsed into a chair, telling Lederlin to keep on talking in case he fell asleep.

'If only we weren't so done in,' he said, 'we might do some surprising things this morning.'

Eventually he was ready to set off again. This time he was accompanied by Raveton, who carried hand grenades. The others were to await their return and keep an eye on the road. 'We're going to try to stop those mortars firing on St-André,' de Buffévent told Raveton and together they disappeared from view, going into the orchards and among the rose trees growing in profusion along the river. They had barely gone when the cadets at the farmhouse saw a German truck pull up on the main road and a platoon of soldiers disembark. It was near the spot where de Buffévent had set the motorcycle on fire; its rider had obviously given the alarm. From the direction in which de Buffévent and Raveton had gone, the cadets at the farmhouse heard the sound of grenades and revolver shots.

'That's the lieutenant,' one of them said, 'in the thick of it.'

The cadets ran back to the river and hid themselves. Then

Lederlin remembered that he had left de Buffévent's fieldglasses at the farmhouse and crept back to retrieve them. There were no more sounds of firing. Lederlin and Douzou then took one of the boats and managed to get back to the island after being fired on in midstream. De Martignac and Thévin had decided to hang on for the return of de Buffévent and Raveton. They waited for an hour but no one came. Then they heard voices shouting in German. De Martignac put his head out and saw a German mortar being put into position some way off.

'It's too far for our grenades,' he told Thévin. He then asked his comrade if he could swim. Thévin said he could not. 'Well, get into the boat and lie down flat,' de Martignac told him.

'What about you?' asked Thévin.

'I'm going into the water and I'll push the boat so that it seems to be drifting empty.'

He took off some of his clothes and they pushed off. At first all seemed to be going well. Then they hit a sandbank and at that moment a bursting shell split the boat, killing Thévin and injuring de Martignac. The boat sank but de Martignac, swimming painfully, eventually reached the south bank and made his way to Lieutenant Périn de St-André's command post by the Cavalry School and told him that de Buffévent and Raveton had disappeared.

It was a long time before they discovered what had happened to them. Gérard de Buffévent and Etienne Raveton had been shot down as they ran through the Jardin des Abeilles which at that time was a mass of red roses. De Buffévent's body was found under one of the rose trees, his head surrounded by its fallen red blossoms.

For the cavalrymen of Saumur the red rose has a special significance. In the *Jeu de la Rose* in the Carrousel, they compete for red roses as their ancestors did in the Middle Ages during the jousts of the knights on the Chardonnet. For a cavalryman of de Buffévent's distinction, to whom the riding events at Saumur meant so much, this end among red roses during the extraordinary Carrousel of June 1940 seemed appropriate. At least that was the view of those who survived him.

The Germans buried de Buffévent and Raveton. The graves were found by those who lived nearby, who came home ten days after the battle, with the armistice signed. By one of the graves was a rough wooden cross on which had been written 'Bufférent – *Französe*' (French). Later there was another rough cross on which had been written: 'His pupils will never forget the hero that he was.' Gérard de Bufférent was posthumously awarded the Legion of Honour. And today, as one drives along the busy road from Saumur along the north bank, one's eye is caught by the slab of stone at the roadside recording that Gérard de Bufférent and Etienne Raveton, instructor and pupil, fell close by on 20 June 1940.

During the night strange things had been going on around Montsoreau at the eastern end of Colonel Michon's sector, where Lieutenant Trastour and the 9th Brigade were on the high ground above the wreck of the iron bridge. Every initiative they took seemed to be known to the Germans in advance: the cadet brigades would be fired on from positions where no Germans were thought to be; at other times the German artillery would mark them with an uncanny accuracy. All this seemed to prove, Colonel Michon noted in his report, the presence in the area of an important spy network. According to the German account, the Army Corps to which the Cavalry Division belonged had a reconnaissance squadron, whose members operated on the south bank of the Loire, sending back information about the movement and strength of French forces and disguising this in language that was flippant, even jokey. Bonnin and Labuzan had with fatal result intercepted two Germans dressed as refugees at the other end of the sector at Gennes. Now at Montsoreau there was more evidence of clandestine activity of German agents in civilian dress.

About 300 metres from Lieutenant Trastour's command post was a villa whose shutters were drawn. It seemed to be deserted. Two days earlier, however, well before the battle began, two men had been intercepted coming from the direction of the house. Their papers were found to be perfectly in order and they were allowed to continue on their way. Later, however, when an inspection of the house was carried out, the cadets discovered not only a plan of the river showing the French positions but also signalling equipment including a gun for firing starshell. Under the villa were vast cellars from which ran passages far down into the cliffs towards the river, providing hidden access to the house.

On the afternoon of 19 June two young men dressed in shorts and singlets were picked up on the river near Dampierre; they were carrying signalling equipment. Taken before Colonel Michon, they said they had come from Paris, that the factory where they worked had been evacuated to Nantes and that they were on their way there. Reaching the Loire, they had been tempted to go on to Nantes by canoe. Then the fighting had started. They had taken shelter with their bicycles in a ditch by the river, and it was there that they had picked up the signalling equipment. Anything might have been possible in the chaos of that hot summer of 1940, even such a story, but Michon found it an unlikely tale and had the two young men sent south under escort.

In the river to the east of the iron bridge at Montsoreau were a number of small islands; from one of these, thought to be uninhabited, had come a sharp burst of rifle fire; it tore across the position on another island where the Algerian riflemen had thought themselves to be hidden, and it came from behind them. Most alarming, however, were the sounds during the night of 19/20 June on the little island of Boiret, where a party of cadets and riflemen were in positions hidden by the thick undergrowth. They had to listen to what sounded like a conversation between blackbirds. Every move they made would be followed by the sound of a blackbird calling; soon after there would be an answering call from a blackbird on the south bank.

One of the cadets recorded how he had set off in the middle of the night on a tour of inspection of the positions on the island: 'Suddenly I was startled by a penetrating whistle. I stopped, thinking I was dreaming. When I set off again, another whistle. It sounded like two or three blackbirds which from different positions were indicating my direction. I had the impression of being followed, of being under a spell.'

For the riflemen on watch, nothing could have been worse. By morning one or two of the Algerian riflemen had been completely unnerved by the 'blackbirds'. They had the impression that the enemy were all round them but invisible. Moreover, the German artillery was firing with an uncanny accuracy, as if the guns were being helped onto their targets by someone on the French side of the river. Targets along the cliffs behind Lieutenant Trastour's command post were being hit persistently. Over towards Saumur they saw the great dome of a beautiful eighteenth-century church, Notre Dame des Ardilliers, collapse in flames, and some way off the historic house Jagenau – where Madame de Montespan, longtime favourite of Louis XIV, had found sanctuary when old and neglected – was twice hit.

Early on the afternoon of Thursday 20 June the German Army Corps commander arrived on the Saumur sector. He could not understand why his cavalry was being held up, why progress was so slow when everywhere else along the Loire his corps was on the move. Angers was in his hands, General de la Laurencie having been ordered to withdraw southward. Even Lyons was in German hands. The General said he had no reinforcements for Saumur: the mounted cavalry would be reaching the Loire shortly, and it was essential that the only bridge still standing, that at Port-Boulet to the east of Montsoreau, should be captured intact to facilitate their passage. However, even before the arrival of the German Army Corps commander, the 22nd Cavalry Regiment had been detached from the Saumur sector with the order to take the bridge at Port-Boulet, the bridge the engineers had failed to destroy and which was causing General Pichon considerable concern. The defence of Port-Boulet was the responsibility of the Dunkirk veteran Colonel du Vigier and his men of the Light Mechanized Division. Colonel Michon's sector ended at Montsoreau bridge but part of his force was operating in liaison with du Vigier's men.

As Thursday 20 June advanced, bringing increasing disarray and confusion along the river, the responsibilities of General Pichon's individual sector commanders became blurred. At midday General Pichon advised the Cavalry School Commandant that Colonel de Vigier would try to 'push towards him some elements of the 3rd DLM' to help him with the defence of Saumur. If the German infiltration to the east and the west of Saumur made it impossible to hold the town and the Cavalry School, he was to pull his cadets out and move them towards Chinon through the forest of Fontevrault.

Colonel Michon had not the slightest intention of giving up: he was in the midst of battle; everywhere his cadets were resisting well. In due course Captain Foltz's message came through, telling him of the success of de Galbert's counter-attack at Gennes. Saumur was still being held; the Cavalry School was intact. However, as Commandant Lemoyne kept telling him, Saumur was now in danger of being taken from its flanks, from the bridgeheads on the south bank that the Germans had been establishing up- and downstream from Saumur since early that morning.

The German Army Corps commander may have found it necessary to complain about the slowness of his cavalry's progress at Saumur but, as he could see himself, his men were across the river. In any case, his complaints and strictures appeared to goad the German cavalry into even more determined effort, and in the afternoon the battle revived with a new intensity on both flanks of Saumur. The cadets, unable to hold their ground, were frequently submerged and casualties were heavy.

The first boats carrying von Edelsheim's men had set off from Villebernier on the north bank to cross over to the little beach below Petit-Puy a few kilometres to the east of Saumur shortly after five o'clock in the morning, after half an hour's heavy shelling from the artillery. They had a difficult task. Getting over the river and onto the beach might be relatively easy but after that they would have to scale the cliffs to get up to Petit-Puy and Dampierre. They did so with great energy. Hubert de la Lance's men by the railway viaduct and the Service Corps cadets of Lieutenant Noirtin did their utmost to stop the invasion but they were constantly harassed by the German cannon firing on them from the north bank. They succeeded in sinking several of the boats in midstream but there were always others, some of them bringing sixteen men at a time. The Germans were simply too strong for the cadets.

Noirtin's brigade of inexperienced Service Corps cadets was decimated; Three were dead; seven others lay wounded and had to be left where they lay as the Germans overran their position and took them prisoner. Hubert de la Lance's cavalry cadets, taken suddenly from the rear, struggled back towards Saumur and rallied at Lieutenant St-Germain's command post at Petit-Puy. De la Lance was hit in the shoulder and, losing a lot of blood, was taken away on a stretcher to a dressing station. St-Germain, his head bandaged, quit Petit-Puy and, forcing a passage through the Germans, got to the outskirts of Saumur, determined to make a last resistance to save the school. He, too, was hit again and this time was taken off to the field ambulance at Marson. Refusing to be anaesthetized, he continued to give his men orders, via a dispatch rider.

Meanwhile Colonel Michon, whose command post at the Auberge de Marsoleau was in striking distance of the Germans now that they were on the cliffs above the Loire, was issuing new orders to meet the serious situation that had arisen since the Germans had got a grip on the south bank of the river. He had already stopped Captain Bleuze and the St-Maixent infantry cadets from proceeding to Gennes in order to help the cavalry cadets trying to stop the Germans advancing from their bridgeheads at Petit-Puy and Dampierre. Now he ordered Second Lieutenant d'Anglejan, the young officer who had been on the island with Gérard de Buffévent and who belonged to Captain de Neuchèze's *Groupe Franc*, to take three of the group's armoured cars and try to attack the Germans from behind.

Three times d'Anglejan patrolled the road between Saumur and Dampierre and with deadly fire drove back the Germans advancing towards Saumur. Two cadets, de la Tour and Humbert, at the head of motorcycle platoons commanded by Lieutenant Surbizy of the de Neuchèze group, rode with the same mad bravery into the enemy positions at Petit-Puy, firing their automatic weapons from sidecars. Cadet Humbert was killed in the fracas but most of his comrades limped away to temporary safety and were able to obey Colonel Michon's order to rally to Captain de St-Blanquat's squadron at Aunis Farm a little to the rear. And to the farm in due course came the St-Maixent infantry cadets.

Amid the growing pressures, Saumur was still holding out. To the west of the town, towards Gennes, Captain Marzolf's squadron, which had started off by being in reserve at Beaucheron, was up on the river trying to stop the Germans getting into the town. On the other side, as has been seen, the Germans were in command of the heights but had not yet reached the château and were not yet in the outskirts of the town.

Inside the town, however, conditions were becoming

Destruction of the suspension bridges at Gennes cut off Desplats's brigade on the island between Gennes and Les Rosiers

With the bridges down, the Germans got across the Loire in rafts but suffered heavy losses

On 19 and 20 June 1940 Saumur was hit by 2,000 shells which shattered many of its ancient buildings, including historic churches

After the battle the Germans built a pontoon bridge over to Saumur

6 July 1940 – Another of Cadet de Navacelle's sketches showing the cadets crossing into Unoccupied France at Loches after being freed by the German general in recognition of their heroism

interpretation of your orders, which, it seems to me, you have already fulfilled. Think again and, if you can, speak about it to your superiors.'

These conversations, conducted in the heart of Saumur as the Germans stood upon its threshold during the afternoon of 20 June 1940, as the French armistice convoy was making its way north to bring hostilities between France and Germany officially to an end, underlined the agonizing moral dilemma confronting ardent and patriotic young spirits in France at that time. The country's father-figure, the venerable Marshal Pétain, had told the country he was seeking an end to the conflict; the Commander-in-Chief, General Weygand, had said, 'Fight on for honour.' And at the same time the Government had prevented the civilian population of Saumur from joining the 9 million Frenchmen already on the roads, refugees from the abandoned battlefields in the north. Saumur's sad significance in June 1940 was that the sacrifice of the cadets, the martyrdom sought by men such as Gérard de Buffévent, was an act of will and the choice of those who were involved, but it could be achieved only by the sacrifice of others who were not consulted and who remain largely unsung.

However, among Saumur's civilians, both men and women, were those who shared the sentiments of the Cavalry School and who worked tirelessly and heroically to succour both the military and the civilians – Abbé François of the religious order of St-Louis, for instance, and Daniel Lacoste. Despite the ever-present dangers of the German bombardment, they went from cellar to cellar with loaves of bread and churns of milk for the families sheltering there. Hour after hour Madame Meulien drove back and forth from Gennes to Doué la Fontaine in her ancient car, taking the wounded to the dressing station. A young girl in trousers and sweater, a refugee from Cherbourg, went from one group of cadets to another taking water and food. When they shouted at her to take cover, she called back that this was the fourth bombardment she had been in. 'Don't worry about me,' she said and ran off to the next barricade.

The unexpected happened. Late on Thursday afternoon, at least one German soldier had succeeded in getting into the town. Seemingly unconcerned, riding a bicycle and carrying a packet, he came riding along the quay leading to the Cavalry

School. Outside a deserted café he stopped, propped up his bicycle and went inside with his packet. Lieutenant Coadic and his cadets, who had been watching his progress, thought he had gone far enough. They went in and took him prisoner. His packet was found to contain sticks of dynamite.

There were those who continued to carry out their duties as if nothing in particular was going on. Madame Victoire of Petit-Puy had no option: in the midst of the battle she gave birth to her tenth child. Madame Beauplet, a nurse, stood by and gave the baby girl as comfortable an entry as was possible into that unpromising world. Civilians who had done their military duty in the First World War retrieved something from their past and were particularly active in bringing comfort and aid to their fellows. Louis Lanoue, once a sergeant in the Colonial Army, having carried supplies to eleven cellars, then drove around in the municipal van, with the town hall caretaker at the wheel, picking up bodies in the street and taking them to the hospital. On the other hand, Henry Fry, disabled in the First World War, decided to stay in bed for the battle and was killed there, a victim of the Second World War.

What had particularly worried the Saumur townsfolk and led to the intervention of their priests was the posting of cadets with automatic weapons and rifles in windows high up in the houses and even among the Gothic masonry of the town hall. The Germans, said the citizens, would regard the cadets as snipers and, as had happened in Spain in the civil war a year or two earlier, reprisals would be taken against the civilian population as if somehow they had been responsible.

In the event, however, there was to be no hand-to-hand fighting in Saumur, no gradual destruction of everything that lay between two opposing forces on a battlefield. By late afternoon on 20 June the Germans had decided, after all, to bypass the town. Their forces were across the Loire just east and west of Saumur and were steadily pushing their way south, despite the efforts of Colonel Michon's men to hold them on the cliffs. It was just a matter of time, they argued, before Saumur would be isolated, when, turning back momentarily, they would take it from the rear. The German intention was to get as far south as possible before the armistice was signed.

Colonel Michon sensed what was happening and prepared to

meet the German drive where it was strongest, where from their bridgehead east of Saumur, east of his command post in the little inn near the Terrefort airfield, they were pushing south away from the Loire at Petit-Puy and Dampierre towards the villages of Champigny, Chaintré, Chacé and Varrains, in whose fields grow the grapes for Saumur's sparkling wines.

Across their path a mile or so from the river stood Aunis Farm, a substantial collection of buildings dating from the end of the sixteenth century, built in the familiar white *tuffeau* stone of Saumur and including barns and stables, the whole surrounded by a substantial stone wall. Here, on Thursday 20 June, Captain de St-Blanquat, coming up from Champigny, had established the command post for the five brigades forming his squadron; here, too, on Colonel Michon's orders, were coming the infantry cadets from St-Maixent and the tanks from Captain de Neuchèze's *Groupe Franc* and even two of Michon's own staff officers to support St-Blanquat. For it was here at Aunis Farm that the Commandant of the Cavalry School and those of his cadets who were still in the battle had decided to make their last stand.

Away down river at Tours by the end of the afternoon the Germans had ordered a cease-fire in their area to enable the French armistice convoy to come over the Loire bridges into their lines. But at 5 p.m., the scheduled time for the crossing, there was no sign of the convoy of ten cars bringing the peace envoys. The Germans began to send off curt messages enquiring what had happened. The delay to General Huntziger's convoy had been caused by the chaotic situation of the roads, blocked for miles by refugee traffic. Eventually the convoy reached General Pichon's sector of the river to the east of Tours. The General was busy fighting his war along the Loire from Azay-le-Rideau, so it was left to the Prefect of the area to get the peace convoy over the river. This was eventually achieved at Amboise at the far end of Pichon's sector. The convoy then picked up a German escort and set off for Paris.

Arriving in the occupied capital during the night they were allowed no rest but instructed to continue north to Compiègne. Here in the railway coach that had been the scene of the 1918 armistice they were to meet Hitler himself. General Huntziger and his delegation, who had been unaware at the start of their journey of where they were to meet the Germans, were shocked to discover what Hitler had planned for them, the theatrical ritual for their humiliation.

After their sleepless night on the roads, they assembled during Friday 21 June at the table in the railway coach and received the German armistice conditions. Huntziger then conveyed them by telephone to General Weygand at Bordeaux; the Germans said they required a reply by nine o'clock the following morning. The exhausted General Huntziger tried to get some rest as at Bordeaux Pétain, Weygand and the rest of the Cabinet remained in permanent session to consider the terms for the armistice. By early the next morning they had still not sent Huntziger their reply; what he did receive was a curt message from General Keitel on the German side which was an ultimatum: the French had one more hour to decide.

At last the telephone rang. It was General Weygand. 'Order is given to the French delegation under General Huntziger to sign the Armistice Agreement. Report when done.' And that was that. General Huntziger said to General Keitel: 'As a soldier you will understand how onerous it is now that the moment has come for me to sign.'

While the French and German military leaders at Compiègne had been going through the protracted exercise to bring hostilities officially to an end, the German Army continued its remorseless advance ever deeper into France – '... despite occasional pockets of resistance with rearguards sacrificing themselves to cover the retreat, and even isolated groups who, having had enough of constantly withdrawing, lay in ambush alongside the roads and met death where they lay,' wrote the French war historian Colonel Goutard. He added: 'The enemy broke down the last resistance on the river despite the efforts of the cadets of the Cavalry School at Saumur who on this day wrote a page of glory into French history.'

5 Aunis Farm – The Last Stand

Captain de St-Blanquat, at thirty-nine years of age already beginning to go grey, was a small, lively man who like Captain Foltz was a cavalry officer of the Reserve. Most of the cadets in his five brigades were about half his age. He had about fifty of them with him at the farm.

Aunis lies on the plateau about a kilometre behind the village of Dampierre and the river, and de St-Blanquat had made his command post there soon after the emergency had begun. Keeping two of his brigades with him, he sent the others to neighbouring farms on either side of Aunis. Like Captain Foltz at Milly-le-Meugon behind Gennes, he was expecting to move up to the river to support the brigades at the bridges when Colonel Michon gave the word. With his brigades spread out on either side of him, he was ready to move left or right as soon as the call came.

Since Aunis Farm would merely be a staging post on the way to joining the battle on the river, nothing was done about preparing the defences of the farm itself. In the event de St-Blanquat was taken by surprise and in the early hours of Thursday 20 June with the Germans across the river at Petit-Puy, he realized that he was caught at the farm. Due to a misunderstanding of orders, he had stayed where he was instead of moving up to the river, as Foltz had at Gennes, once it was clear that the German attempt to cross the river, upstream and downstream from Saumur, had started.

Aunis had suddenly become a strategic target for the Germans who, now that they were over the river, would have to come over its farmlands, through its orchards, its fields of wheat and its vineyards, as they struck out towards the south. If they were to be stopped, the farmhouse and its surrounding outbuildings would have to be transformed into a fortress. De St-Blanquat's men went to work. Trenches were dug hurriedly along the road to the farm, and the earth was piled up in places to give the impression that anti-tank mines were in place. The roads into the nearby village of Champigny were blocked with one or two old cars whose tyres had been deflated. Machine-guns and automatic rifles were carried up to windows on the upper storey of the farmhouse and even onto the roof. Two cadets on watch with binoculars reported seeing men in shirtsleeves and black trousers moving towards the farm. The Germans were firing starshell as signals that the French could not understand. Their aircraft flew over, and soon after that the German artillery on the other side of the river went into action, giving the French the impression that the aircraft were directing the big guns onto their targets.

De St-Blanquat, meanwhile, had sent word to his brigades in the outlying positions to which he had previously sent them, to get back to Aunis as quickly as they could. They, however, were already at grips with the enemy, having taken the initiative in going after the mortars that were firing on the farm. Lieutenant Gand was killed as he led the 13th Brigade across a wheatfield towards one of the German guns; his NCO Richebé also fell, wounded. A minute later Cadets Prat and Bodot were killed, but still their comrades went forward. Lieutenant Wrede of the German cavalry recorded: 'The cadets of the Cavalry School of Saumur got to within 150 metres of their objective with an utter contempt for death, trying again and again to gain ground and renewing their attack.' Among the cadets of Lieutenant Gand's brigade who attacked the Germans with a fanatical zeal was Pierre Delafon, known to his comrades as '*le grand Bill*', an enormous young man with a great eagle-like nose and possessed of great strength. Again and again he went into the attack, knocking out seven of his assailants and at the same time keeping up a shouted barrage of insults 'drawn from a repertoire that seemed inexhaustible'.

Two of the cadets in the 14th Brigade, commanded by Lieutenant the Comte de St-Pol, reported they were so close to the Germans that they could hear the enemy's officers giving orders. St-Pol was trying to head back westwards towards the farm but in the murderous German fire from the mortars they were constantly having to take cover and could make little progress. Lieutenant the Comte Martin de Marolles with the 16th Brigade had had to hole up in a disused quarry, unable to get across the German line of fire and back to Aunis.

From Aunis Farm itself came the constant rattle of machine-gun fire. De St-Blanquat's cadets were giving the German positions everything they had. The reappearance among them of the Jesuit priest, Instructor Lieutenant Lucien Fraisse, had given their morale a boost. Fraisse had earlier had to hand over command of the 15th Brigade to Lieutenant Gantois on account of illness but during the night he had turned up again from no one knew where, leaving his sickbed behind and resuming his duties. 'A great joy to have him back,' one of his cadets recorded. 'His calm, his authority, his fighting qualities strengthened us.' Whatever it was, the farm was putting up a tremendous resistance and the Germans were worried. According to Sergeant Peters of the German engineers, the 3rd German Cavalry Squadron had sent back a message to their heavy artillery to destroy the farm as it was holding up their advance. However, the German field guns never succeeded in putting the farm out of action; it was the fire from the mortars and small cannon that eventually set the buildings alight.

East of Aunis Farm, at his command post at the Auberge de Marsoleau, Colonel Michon, realizing that de St-Blanquat was in trouble, took immediate steps to get help to him. As with Foltz at Gennes, there was only one recipe in Michon's book when disaster threatened: order a counter-attack. 'Hold on as best you can,' he told de St-Blanquat. 'A counter-attack is on its way.'

Captain Bleuze, in charge of the company of infantry cadets from St-Maixent, was ordered to undertake the counter-attack from the village of Chacé, south of Aunis Farm. Here, after a night on the roads being sent hither and thither, first towards Foltz at Gennes, then back again towards Saumur, they had arrived early on the morning of 20 June. Bleuze was told that Captain de Neuchèze was sending from his *Groupe Franc* one of his crack officers, Lieutenant Alain Pitiot, in command of five Hotchkiss tanks, to clear a path for the infantry charge. He sent two of his own staff officers, Captain Delmotte and Lieutenant de Gaillard de Lavaldène, to help Bleuze direct the attack.

Cadet Toulemonde embarked both these officers on his motorcycle at the same time, and they reached Bleuze at Chacé without mishap. Almost immediately a messenger arrived from de St-Blanquat to say that the situation at Aunis was critical and asking that the counter-attack be made without delay.

The farm buildings were burning but still the cadets had not abandoned their posts; they were trying to put out the flames with a fire-extinguisher from the old farm Renault and they threw on water and sand. They kept up their own firing on the Germans advancing from Dampierre, some of whom had mounted weapons in the apple trees to hit back at the cadets.

The battle was taking its toll on the defenders. Cadet Gaston André, having fired his red-hot rifle for nearly six hours, was eventually hit in the head and died in captivity the next day. The wounded were carried down into the cellar of the farmhouse, where Cadet Paravisini, who had been a medical student when the war started, was doing his best to help his comrades.

The cowman, old Joseph Darnaud, the only farmworker still around, had been a sergeant in 1914. When it seemed that a battle was to take place, not having his old uniform he changed into his best suit, the one he wore on Sundays, and never ceased to help the young cavalry cadets who had suddenly come into his life. He brought them drinks and food, carried ammunition, brought the wounded down into the cellar. For his tireless efforts at Aunis Farm that day he was to be mentioned in dispatches and awarded the Croix de Guerre.

'About 1300 hours the situation became untenable. Aunis was a real hell,' one of its defenders wrote later. 'Flying over the farm at low altitude, aircraft fired on its defenders while the bombardment continued without a stop and the grip of the enemy tightened. But morale was high and we were convinced we would get out of it.'

They would get out only if help came soon. De St-Blanquat's brigades that had been out in the fields had made a brave but vain attempt to get back to the farm, whose defenders were becoming fewer as the battle took its toll. Meanwhile, the Germans had mounted a new assault from a different direction, the north-west, and if they were not stopped, they would be able to get round the back of the farm and effectively surround it. It was in this direction, therefore, that the counter-attack promised by Colonel Michon would have to go.

Lieutenant Alain Pitiot was ready. A brave young officer, he had already performed acts of great daring in the battles on the Somme and on the Seine with de Neuchèze's *Groupe Franc.* Now he led his five Hotchkiss tanks out of the village of Chaintré behind the farm. His mission was to sweep the ground to the north-west to clear a passage to enable Bleuze and his St-Maixent infantry cadets to make their bayonet charge against the Germans who, advancing from Beaulieu, were threatening to surround the farm. In the narrow street through Chaintré Pitiot's little force looked quite formidable; his own tank had lost its turret but it proudly flew its leader's command pennant. Pitiot, bareheaded, was standing erect, half of him unprotected, but he quite oblivious of danger. He went with that 'calm and serene grandeur' for which he was known, said one of his comrades. But he was very vulnerable.

Once out in the open, the enemy guns soon picked them up. They kept on in face of intense fire and came abreast of the farm on their right. Calmly Pitiot gave the signal for the tanks to fan out, side by side, for the attack. But it was soon over. The German anti-tank barrage was deadly. Pitiot, standing up to fire his gun, was cut in half by a German shell fired at a range of thirty metres. The tank next to him was hit and its engine put out of action; its crew, instead of abandoning it, continued to fire their gun until suddenly the whole tank went up in flames and two men with it. The three surviving tanks managed to get themselves out of range.

By now Captain Bleuze and his infantry cadets had gone in with shouts of elation and were firing away as they came across the fields and reached the farm. Infantry cadets and cavalry cadets – the '*compagnons d'armes*' of the official report – were now mixed up, fighting side by side, shoulder to shoulder. For a while they succeeded in holding the German onslaught but by now the Germans had so many of their men over the river that it could be only a matter of time before the defenders of Aunis would be overwhelmed.

In the living-room of the farm de St-Blanquat with Colonel Michon's staff officers, Delmotte and de Gaillard de Lavaldène took stock of their situation. The counter-attack had momentarily dented the pocket of the German advance but the bombardment from the German guns and machine-gun attack from their aircraft had made their continuing presence in the farm increasingly perilous.

A barn full of hay was burning; incendiary shells had set a second barn on fire, and the cadets had barely had time to get the cows and a terrified horse out into the open. The heat of the flames, combined with the heat of the sun, had brought the surviving cadets to a state of exhaustion but their morale seemed unaffected. One of them, when told by de St-Blanquat to come down from the roof where he had been firing his weapon for hours, was able to reply: '*Mon capitaine*, when one has the honour to be up here, one only comes down when dead.' That had already been the fate of too many of his comrades at Aunis.

Down in the cellar there was barely room for another wounded soldier. Medical supplies had run out. Up top they were also running out of ammunition. The roof of the farmhouse looked as if it were going to fall in – de St-Blanquat and the other officers finished their deliberations outside behind the farm wall.

In the middle of the afternoon, they decided to pull out while the routes south to Chaintré and Chacé were still open. A cadet ran down to the cellar and called out to Octave Paravisini, 'We're pulling out. The Germans are here.' Lieutenant Monéger, who, like Lucien Fraisse, was a priest, moved among the dying, performing the Last Rites. Then, becoming a soldier again, he picked up an automatic rifle that had been left behind and, like the rest of them, set off for the assembly place – appropriately enough, the Calvary at Chaintré. Cadet Paravisini was not prepared to leave his wounded comrades.

'The firing above our heads became sporadic,' he recorded. 'Then there was a great silence. I saw Noack arrive – he's Alsatian. "They're here," he said. "Put your arms down at the entrance to the cellar." Then there was the sound of boots, guttural shouts, curt orders and then rifles appeared at the entrance pointing at us. An officer came in. He looked round the cellar. I saw clearly on his face an expression of stupefaction. "All these wounded," he seemed to be saying, "and the dead that I don't know about." He said something in German that I did not understand.'

Noack, the Alsatian, understood: '*Kavalleriekadetten. Tapfere soldaten*,' he was saying. 'Cavalry Cadets. Brave soldiers.'

Cadet Paravisini explained that only the wounded remained at Aunis Farm. Cadets who had been brought in as prisoners by the Germans helped to carry the wounded up from the cellar. 'We came out of the cellar between two rows of Germans who stood to attention,' Paravisini recorded.

The Germans, now in command at Aunis Farm, looked back towards Petit-Puy and Dampierre on the banks of the Loire from which they had come. It was a scene of utter desolation: shattered branches of trees, broken walls of stone, fallen telephone wires, wire fences that had been used to keep animals in the fields lying across roads pitted by the shells fired by German guns on the north bank. Unmilked cows wandered pitifully from place to place, untended.

The Germans, with their French prisoners, went out to pick up the dead from the fields and orchards. Bodies lay grotesquely where they had fallen. One, caught in a tree, was still standing, a horrifying and menacing sight, fingers still gripping the rifle. They found the body of the young French composer and organist Jéhan Allain. He was just beginning to make a reputation when the war started. Having served in Flanders and won the Croix de Guerre, he had been at Dunkirk and was one of those who had got back to France from Britain in time to take part in the fighting on the Loire at Saumur, acting as a dispatch rider. Seeing a German force approaching, he had abandoned his motorcycle and sidecar and from a trench near the farm had taken on the Germans with his automatic rifle. When his ammunition ran out, he made a dash for his motorcycle but was hit when he got there. Later, in the upturned sidecar, they found sheets of music he had been working on.

In due course the defence of Aunis Farm by the Cavalry Cadets of Saumur and their companions in arms, the Infantry Cadets of St-Maixent, on 20 June 1940, acquired a special significance in the legends of Saumur. It has been referred to as '*La Haie Sainte*' ('The Sacred Line') by those who remembered that, exactly 125 years earlier, almost to the day and the hour, the French had made another brave but vain defence of a farmhouse – on the battlefield at Waterloo. Today, where the dust road from the farm meets the highway going east from Saumur, there is a little stone monument that recalls the battle that was fought there on 20 June 1940; it commemorates the names of François Gand, Alain Pitiot and their fallen comrades.

The defence of Aunis Farm was the last organized resistance made by Colonel Michon and his cadets along the sector of the river that had been allotted to them by General Pichon. Early on the afternoon of 20 June the General had sent his liaison officer, Captain Dujardin, to see Colonel Michon and take stock of the situation. On receiving Dujardin's report of the perilous situation now facing the Cavalry School in its effort to hold Saumur, General Pichon decided that enough was enough. At the end of the afternoon Colonel Michon received formal instructions to disengage his forces and to withdraw them south and east towards Fontevrault and the Vienne river.

General Pichon had taken this step, in his own words, '... because of the general situation on the Loire and concerned not to have massacred needlessly at Saumur the entire élite of the young Cavalry'. The 'general situation on the Loire' to which he referred was the breaking of the French resistance all along the river – already the civil authorities at Chinon and Langlais had appealed to him to give up the fight. However, he decided to withdraw only after hearing that General Héring's Army of Paris had escaped encirclement and was on its way to safety in what became the Unoccupied Zone.

At nine o'clock that evening Pichon gave a general order to withdraw from the Loire but not in time to stop one final battle at the bridges, to the east of Colonel Michon's sector, at Port-Boulet.

At that hour the Germans' 22nd Cavalry Regiment made their attempt to seize the bridge that was still intact, having survived the efforts of the French engineers to destroy it. The bridge had been a major problem for Colonel du Vigier defending it and for General Pichon himself. The first attempt to destroy the bridge – on 19 June – had only damaged it. Another attempt, in the early hours of 20 June, had caused one arch to collapse but it was still possible for light vehicles to cross. Pichon asked the Air Force to bomb it; this was agreed for 5 p.m., then postponed and finally cancelled. There was no sign of the French Air Force at Saumur. Once during the battle a Potez flew high overhead, but it did not intervene. At Port-Boulet the bridge remained for the taking. One of those present when the battle started at nine o'clock on the evening of

20 June was Sergeant Peters of the 40th Battalion of German engineers. 'The south bank of the Loire,' he wrote, 'was occupied by the enemy. According to statements made by prisoners, there were some pupils of the Cavalry School who were determined to fight on to the end.' The German 5th Squadron, said Peters, despite a terrific fire from the French, got over to the south bank without too much trouble. 'But on the left, it was another matter. In the attacking zone of the 6th Squadron were a number of little islands occupied by the enemy and which slowed down considerably the crossing of the river and where the squadron had some losses.'

'At 2300 hours,' Peters went on, 'after the German pioneers had cleared the obstacles at the entrance to the bridge, the 7th Squadron went into the attack on the bridge but struck a tremendous resistance which they were not able to overcome until the 5th Squadron, the most advanced of those already on the south bank, took the French from behind. But the enemy defended himself with determination and in the dark often passed behind our cavalrymen and fired on their backs. On 21 June at thirty minutes past midnight the Germans finally overcame the French defenders and took them prisoner.'

The bridge was intact and in the hands of the 22nd Cavalry Regiment, which, following the orders of the Army Corps commander, set off not for Saumur but for Chinon, in order to get a bridgehead over the Cher river and go in pursuit of the French armies withdrawing to the east of them.

But it was really all over. As one of those who took part in the German victory, General von Mellentin, recorded, the closing stages of the 1940 campaign in France were reminiscent of the French Cavalry pursuit over the plains of northern Germany after Napoleon's victory at the battle of Jena. The position of the German Panzers in France in June 1940 was similar to that outlined by Prince Murat in his message to Napoleon: 'Sire, the fighting is over, because there are no more combatants left.'

Nine o'clock on the evening of 20 June was also the decisive hour for Colonel Michon, for it was only then that he finally decided to abandon Saumur and the Cavalry School to the Germans.

Several hours earlier, when he had received General Pichon's order to withdraw from the Loire, Michon's immediate response was to say that he would go himself to Azay-le-Rideau to try to get the General to change his mind. He could not bring himself to accept an order to retreat. 'We're holding on,' he kept saying to Commandant Lemoyne, his chief of staff, and Captain Delmotte, who was back after Aunis Farm had been abandoned. 'We're holding on, heroically,' he insisted.

Lemoyne had not only to study how best to get his surviving cadets safely away to the assembly point in the forest; he had also patiently to make his colonel see reason. Nearly two days without rest, the constant pain of his old wounds and the pressing need for quick decisions as the situation changed along the river, never knowing where the Germans would attempt another crossing, had exhausted the old soldier. Michon was unable to face up to the reality of his situation, and yet General Pichon's words about the unnecessary massacring of the young élite of the Cavalry, his own cadets, had affected him deeply.

In Michon's mind was fixed the image of his personal runner, Cadet Fouquet-Lemaître. Backwards and forwards he had gone, day and night, doing what the telephone and radio ought to have been doing, linking the Colonel and his forces. He usually went by motorcycle, sometimes on foot. He had carried the Commandant's orders to Aunis Farm earlier in the day. Back at the inn he stood before the Colonel as usual, stiffly to attention. He saluted and said, 'Aunis is holding out.' He handed Michon a packet of notes which were dirty and bloodstained. He started to give a further message verbally. But something was wrong. He was deathly white. His words came slowly, then suddenly he collapsed in a heap. It was only then they noticed that his right arm had been shattered. Fouquet-Lemaître had run the gauntlet for the last time. On the way back from Aunis Farm his motorcycle had been knocked out and he himself wounded. He was picked up by a colleague with a motorcycle and sidecar and brought to the Auberge de Marsoleau.

The picture of the white-faced cadet, swaying on his feet as he gave his message, had remained with his colonel. The sacrifice of so many of his pupils and their instructors seemed to him to require of their Commandant a personal sacrifice of his own. At one moment Michon began to speak wildly of going back alone to his quarters in the Cavalry School; he would

The window in the church at Milly-le-Meugon depicting the cadets' armed vigil during the night of 19 June 1940

'To the memory of the Cadets of Saumur and their Companions-at-Arms'. Graves of the fallen at St-Eusèbe church, Gennes

General the Comte de Galbert DSO, an instructor lieutenant in 1940, Commandant of the Cavalry School in 1965 and later Governor of *Les Invalides* in Paris

Lieutenant Desplats is commemorated by a 1940 armoured car in front of the Cavalry School

change into full dress uniform and, revolver in hand, stand in the entrance to the school to await the Germans – and his own end. Was this what the Roman senators had done when the Barbarians approached, what General Weygand had wished upon the Reynaud Government in Paris? Lemoyne, eminently sensible, and another staff officer, Lieutenant Puzenet, brought Michon back to earth. Practical steps were needed, not melodramatic gestures. If the Colonel would move his men out now, as instructed by General Pichon, not only would he avoid the destruction of the little island of resistance but, by regrouping on another line to the south, they would actually prolong the resistance of the Cavalry School. The Colonel lay down on a bench to ease his aching body and to think.

At 9 p.m. Michon got up and ordered the disengagement of all his men along the sector, instructing them to assemble during the night at Roiffé, seven kilometres south of Fontevrault Abbey on the main road to Poitiers. But what to do with himself? For an hour he sat in the car, with Captain de Neuchèze at the wheel, unable to bring himself to quit the battlefield and the sector of the Loire he had been given to defend. By morning, he thought, the Germans would be in the Cavalry School. In the end he gave a weary nod to de Neuchèze and they drove off into the night, Michon perhaps already formulating the words of his report.

'The movement,' he was to write, 'began at 21.30 throughout the sector, at Gennes, at Saumur and at Montsoreau, the losses are heavy, all the reserves were engaged, the lack of artillery was cruelly felt, but on the whole the sector holds.' But at what a price!

It was dark when, from Gennes in the west to Montsoreau in the east, all Colonel Michon's young men who were still in the fight began to move away from the battlefield. Captain Foltz was still holding the streets of Gennes, and Albert de Galbert, after his earlier counter-attacking exploits, had taken refuge in a building with his men. 'We'll spend the night here,' he told them, 'and at dawn we'll make a quick raid with grenades and bring in some prisoners.' Then he stretched out in an armchair, putting his feet on another. Like Turenne and Joffre, de Galbert had the ability to go to sleep between battles. They had to wake him to give him the news of the withdrawal order from Colonel

Michon. 'What a pity they didn't leave us alone,' he said. 'We might have had some fun in the morning!'

Over the river at Les Rosiers, the Mayor and the priest Abbé Gaultier were still being held in the square. The Mayor's wife and daughter had been allowed to come and talk to them. Eventually a German Protestant chaplain intervened and secured their release. The Germans, meanwhile, had about fifty prisoners assembled in the church, and the Mayor and priest, despite their fatigue, went round taking their names and addresses so that they could write to their families.

German losses in the fighting around Gennes and Les Rosiers had been high – between 200 and 300 casualties. They themselves paid tribute to the quality of the defenders. 'We had to kill them twice,' said one of the German officers. On Friday 22 June the Barrau sisters, who kept the Hôtel de la Loire, were out in the street examining the damage to their property when a German officer approached them.

'Who were the troops defending the bridges?' he asked.

'The pupils and officers of Saumur,' they said, 'with some North African soldiers.'

'Be proud of them,' the German said. 'They were heroes.'

For these heroes, however, the fight had not finished. Captain Foltz, de Galbert and others of the squadron had the longest distance to travel to reach the assembly point behind Fontevrault at the other end of the sector. During the night, after looking around for other squadrons, they halted at Doué la Fontaine, and in the morning Foltz decided to go it alone and keep on fighting. This they did, as will be seen, right up till the signing of the armistice on 23 June, the day of the last battle, when their ammunition ran out.

In Saumur itself, still in French hands, the call to disengage found Lieutenant Périn de St-André and his men without transport to get themselves to Roiffé. At once they went in search of bicycles, taking them wherever they found them, men's bicycles, women's bicycles, bicycles of the *belle époque*, bicycles of every period, bicycles of every conceivable kind. It was a strange procession that took the road out of Saumur, cadets of the celebrated Cavalry School and its equally celebrated riding school, mounted on every shape and size of bicycle. And since the Germans who had got across the river at

Petit-Puy and, taking Aunis Farm, had penetrated several kilometres south of Saumur, to reach their destination in the east they had to take a long, roundabout route.

Away in the east, behind Montsoreau, Lieutenant Trastour's brigade was also riding bicycles. These they had found at Fontevrault, which they had reached on foot, being but a short distance from their battle station at the iron bridge. They had crept silently away from the river without apparently attracting the attention of the Germans, which was, in any case, engaged further east where the battle for the bridge at Port-Boulet was in progress. Trastour's cadets, with the shortest distance to travel, were among the first to reach Roiffé. There, finding a barn filled with hay, they threw themselves down and slept and slept.

6 Exodus of the Horses

The battle between the German Cavalry Division and France's Cavalry cadets had been fought at Saumur without horses. The battle was over by the time the mounted elements of the German Cavalry, after two days in the saddle, reached the Loire. In the early hours of 21 June, shortly after their motorized comrades had won possession of the bridge at Port-Boulet, they rode over it to the south bank of the river.

The French Cavalry cadets who formed the five brigades of Lieutenant de St-Germain's squadron and who had defended the bridges would normally have been mounted; they had been transported to their battle stations in military vehicles and, when the order came to pull out, had left the scene on bicycles. The French horses, 800 of them, had left the Cavalry School in a convoy going south on the morning of 18 June, led by one of France's most distinguished riders of the 1930s, Colonel de Laissardière. By the early hours of Friday 21 June, when the Germans took the bridge at Port-Boulet, enabling their own horsemen to cross the Loire, and when the resistance ended along the Saumur sector, the French horses, after two days on the road, ought to have been well south and out of danger of falling into German hands. But were they?

At first the movement towards the south had gone well enough. They reached La Motte-Chandenier during the afternoon and called a halt. That night they heard the explosions at Saumur when the bridges were blown up, and at six o'clock the next morning, 19 June, they were *en route* for Thénezay and the forest of Autun. Before them was a ride of some sixty kilometres.

Colonel de Laissardière's mounted convoy set off first and was followed half an hour later by the motorized column led by

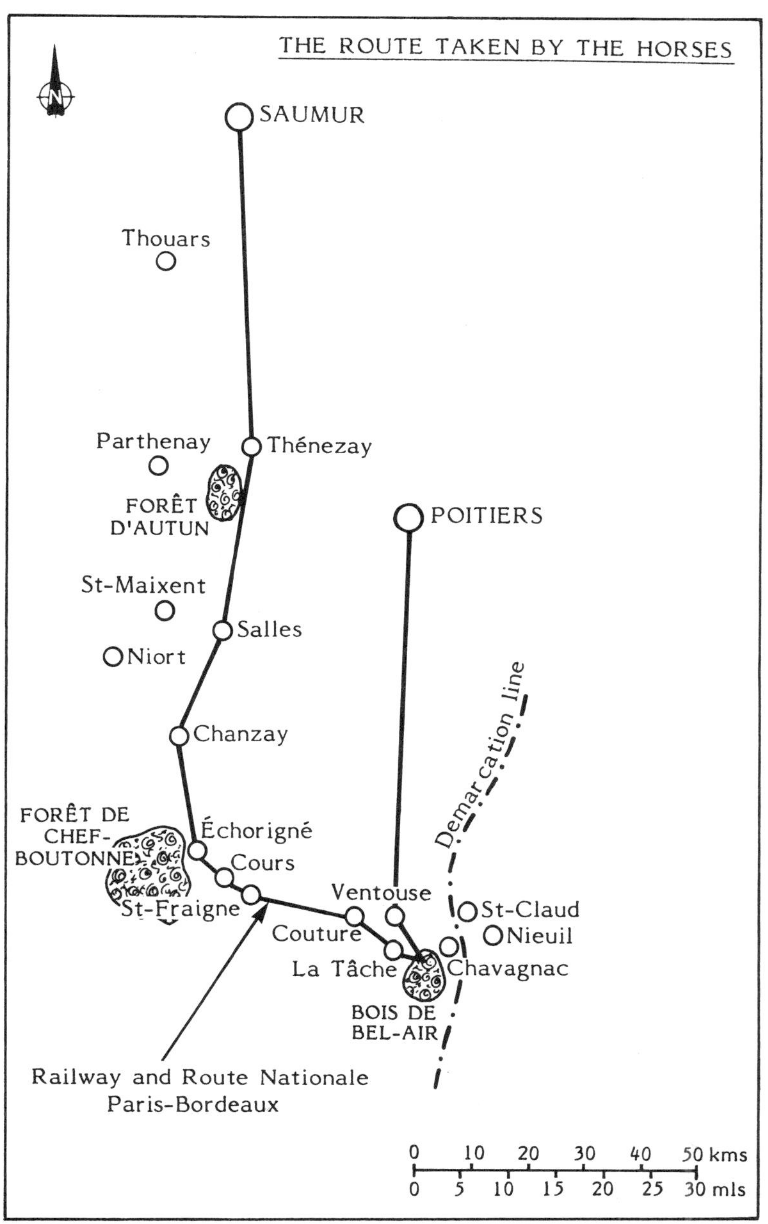
THE ROUTE TAKEN BY THE HORSES
N
SAUMUR
Thouars
Parthenay
Thénezay
FORÊT D'AUTUN
POITIERS
St-Maixent
Salles
Niort
Demarcation line
Chanzay
FORÊT DE CHEF-BOUTONNE
Échorigné
Cours
St-Fraigne
Ventouse
St-Claud
Nieuil
Couture
La Tâche
Chavagnac
BOIS DE BEL-AIR
Railway and Route Nationale Paris-Bordeaux
0 10 20 30 40 50 kms
0 5 10 15 20 25 30 mls

Colonel Massiet, who was transporting in his trucks all that was valuable and important to the Cavalry School and which ought not to fall into enemy hands. By five o'clock that afternoon the convoy, both mounted and mechanized, was encamped in the forest of Autun next to the Comte de Talhouet's hunting lodge, whose single waterpump had to serve the entire company of men and horses.

Colonel Massiet, who had overall command of the evacuation, then decided that it would be best if the two parts of the convoy, his own motorized section and Colonel de Laissardière's mounted section, should continue their journey separately and independently. His cars and trucks were being held up by the need to follow the horses, and with the uncertainties of the rapidly changing war situation, he felt he should not delay his own progress. In the morning he said goodbye to Laissardière and, taking the Cavalry School standard in his own car, set off. For Massiet there were no more problems: on 22 June, with his convoy, he reported to the Director of Cavalry at Montauban.

Montauban was also the destination of de Laissardière and the horses but his was to be a much more difficult journey. He called a meeting of his officers and NCOs, who were joined by the three cadets who were part of his team. They discussed a plan of action. There were 559 men in the convoy, 827 horses and fifty-five horse-drawn vehicles. Among the horses were seventy that had come to France from Canada and which, having arrived at Saumur only the previous March, were still not fully trained and were causing problems for the young officer in charge of them. Some of the horses were tired, others had lost shoes. Some of the horses pulling the waggons were restless and stubborn in harness. When the convoy was assembled and on the move, it stretched for five kilometres. Along the roads it became entangled with the hordes of refugees and scattered bands of soldiers. De Laissardière and his officers decided that in order to simplify the convoy, to increase its mobility, they would have to get rid of some of the waggons. These had been overloaded and already they had had to disembark some of the cargo at the town hall at Thénezay. At St-Maixent, site of the Infantry School whose cadets had made the bayonet charge at Aunis Farm, they found a suitable place to leave some of the waggons. De Laissardière would have preferred to abandon all his waggons, since his one concern was the safety of the horses – the waggons were only holding them up.

On 22 June they were encamped at Salles, not far from St-Maixent, but when word reached them that German motorcyclists had entered St-Maixent, they quickly moved off again. The following evening, when they learned from the radio that General Huntziger had signed the armistice document at Réthondes, they were at Chanzay. According to the armistice conditions, hostilities would cease six hours after a similar armistice with the Italians had been signed. Marshal Pétain had given orders that meanwhile all French military formations should stay where they were.

The Germans seemed to be moving about all over the place, and Colonel de Laissardière wondered how long it would be before they discovered his convoy of horses. A new complication was that a number of fleeing Frenchmen, both soldiers and civilians, had attached themselves to the convoy, asking to be fed and to be taken along with the horses. The Colonel looked at his map: the demarcation line that would separate Occupied France from what was to be the Unoccupied Zone of the future Vichy France was within striking distance, not much more than about seventy kilometres. Could he possibly cover that distance without being seen by the roving patrols of the German military? He took another look at the horses. Here were some of his old favourites, horses he had ridden in international events in London and Paris, even in Berlin. It was unthinkable that he should allow them to become a war trophy for the victorious Germans.

On the morning of 24 June the column was concealed in the forest of Chef Boutonne, just south of the village of Échorigné. Soon after midday they saw a column of German motorcyclists going by without apparently noticing them. Then a German plane flew over. In the evening the radio announced that the armistice with the Italians had been signed. That meant that hostilities would cease the next morning at four o'clock. De Laissardière decided that he would move the column at seven o'clock – that is, three hours after hostilities had ended, just to make certain that they really had. They would make for the village of Cours about twenty kilometres away – this would get them away from the big roads where they were most likely to encounter German columns.

At Cours they hid once more in the woods. That evening, when the Colonel attended rollcall as usual, he explained to the assembled men what their situation was. Only seventy kilometres now separated them from the Free Zone. Once over the demarcation line, they would be safe. On the other hand, if they were intercepted by the Germans, he could not see the victors allowing the horses of the Cavalry School of Saumur to pass out of their hands. How should they go? Ride at night? With so many inexperienced riders and some who were not riders at all, they would certainly lose themselves, but to ride in broad daylight was to invite attention. De Laissardière had thought of going to the German Area HQ at Angoulême to seek a safe conduct, but that, he decided, was too risky; he had no confidence that the Germans would let the horses go. In several places he had been told by the *gendarmerie* that, despite the armistice, the Germans were still taking prisoners.

De Laissardière then decided to go and see the French military commanders at Périgueux and Limoges to see what advice they could give. One of his young officers, Second Lieutenant Roques, had his own car with the convoy – a sports-car enthusiast, he had been unable to bring himself to leave it behind at Saumur for the pleasure of the Germans. The Colonel borrowed it and drove off at speed, first to Périgueux, where he saw a colonel, then to Limoges, where he was received by a general. Neither felt able to help him. A kind of inertia was setting in, and de Laissardière could see that he alone would have to deal with the problem of moving 500 men, 800 horses and fifty-five vehicles a distance of seventy kilometres without being seen by the Germans.

The task seemed barely possible, and his officers were pessimistic. Lieutenant Roques, the sports-car enthusiast, had the particular responsibility of feeding men and horses. Where, he wondered, was he going to find 3,000 kilos of hay, 5,000 kilos of oats, 450 kilos of bread, 300 kilos of meat?

Throughout 27 June and the following day they remained where they were. Some of the men, putting on civilian clothes, went out in search of nourishment for men and horses. They returned pushing well-laden farm carts. Colonel de Laissardière

enter the Unoccupied Zone. The Germans replied that they knew nothing about what had been in the newspapers; they had their orders to stop the convoy, and there was no option but to obey them. De Laissardière then asked to be taken to the general commanding the area and, getting into their car, he drove with the German officers to the general's headquarters. The general was out. De Laissardière then tried to convince his chief-of-staff, but he was not prepared to take the responsibility of releasing the Cavalry School's men and horses. Later that evening the whole of the column was moved away from the demarcation line, first to Ventouse and then back to Poitiers, where it was accommodated in the former artillery base.

For Colonel de Laissardière, who had got his men and horses to within a kilometre of the Free Zone and had actually stood there, a free man, it was a bitter disappointment. At Poitiers the Germans offered him his freedom but he refused it; he did, however, accept a *laisser-passer* so that he could return briefly to Saumur to reassure himself of the safety of his wife and family, who had been there during the fighting. In any case, he had not given up the struggle to save the horses. For him, as for any equerry of the *Cadre Noir*, those horses had a significance as important as the standard of the Cavalry School itself, now safely at Montauban. To reassemble them once more under the standard was still his purpose and in the days ahead he would use all his powers of persuasion, all the influence that his personal reputation as a champion horseman could command, to prevent the horses of the *Cadre Noir* being removed to Germany.

7 Armistice and Aftermath

It was the morning of 21 June, and in Saumur a German cavalry colonel was speaking to Monsieur Ancelin, the town's magistrate.

'I came here as a young officer years ago,' the colonel was saying, 'to take part in the riding events. I used to go around with Lieutenant Bizard, Captain de Laissardière, Lieutenant Aublet ... it's a sad business, war.'

The Germans had entered the town at 7.30 that morning, driving along the heights past the Villa des Grandes Brises, where Colonel Michon had had his first command post, on past the Château de Saumur and then down the steep incline into the town centre. Monsieur Ancelin was out in the streets surveying the scene of desolation that his town presented after two days of battle. The Germans stopped and spoke to him. 'Where is the Cavalry School?' they asked. The magistrate indicated the direction they should take but they suggested that he should go with them. 'We want to be certain there are no more French soldiers here,' he was told. In the next few days senior German officers visited the school again and again; it seemed to have a fascination for them, and they would not allow their own men to occupy it.

While a German colonel and a French magistrate were speaking of a happier past, in the forest of Fontevrault officers and pupils of the school were having to cope with a present that was becoming ever more chaotic. Throughout the night men and machines had been arriving at Roiffé from all directions and from a variety of units, not just those from Colonel Michon's force. There was extreme confusion, and Michon's two staff officers, Delmotte and de Gaillard de Lavaldène, who earlier had taken part in the fighting at Aunis Farm, had the utmost difficulty in trying to restore some sort of order among the cadet brigades.

At two o'clock in the morning of 21 June General Pichon's liaison officer, Lieutenant Dujardin, arrived. He was looking for Colonel Michon but no one knew where he was. Dujardin said he had heard that the Commandant of the Cavalry School was out looking for General Pichon and had gone in the direction of Chinon. But Chinon, he said, was already in German hands. (In fact, the St-Maixent infantry cadets with Captain Bleuze were prisoners there. As they had arrived at Chinon, all unsuspecting, in their transports, the Germans had picked them off, one by one, like fruit off a tree.) Dujardin had brought new instructions for Colonel Michon and the Cavalry School brigades. They were to go further east, to Lerné, on the edge of the forest, where they should hide, out of sight of enemy aircraft, and wait there until the armistice was signed.

Two hours later the cadets were encamped in the grounds of the Château de Chavigny at Lerné. Many of them had made a bed for themselves in the hay in the barns of the farm buildings of the château. Captain Marzolf's squadron, which had come a long way from a position well west of Saumur over towards Gennes and had been marching all night, arrived just before 5 a.m. His cadets sank down under the trees, on the moss, on the dead leaves, and slept where they lay.

At that moment Colonel Michon himself turned up, with Captain de Neuchèze, in a motorcycle and sidecar, after hours of fruitless searching for General Pichon. Although it was a warm night, Michon had a red blanket round his shoulders and was shivering with exhaustion. The sight of his cadets thrown together in the crowded park of the château with the ragged remnants of other units, with civilians who had arrived there in trucks, made him feel even worse. They gave him the dispatch that Lieutenant Dujardin had brought from General Pichon.

'You know,' he said to de Gaillard de Lavaldène, 'that General Pichon has authorized the surrender of the school with the aim of sparing the blood of our heroic youth. Here are his actual words.' Holding up the paper, he went on: ' "The armistice is near. Try to camouflage yourselves in the woods as long as possible but, if you are discovered, surrender without fighting in order not to sacrifice an élite of which France is going to have the greatest need."' Colonel Michon put down his general's dispatch. 'However,' he said, 'I do not wish to be caught by the enemy in this frightful mess. I don't wish to preside over this chaos, this mix-up of all these units where my own pupils are just a minority.'

Once again he began to talk of going back alone to the Cavalry School to wait for the Germans. Again his officers dissuaded him, telling him that it was too late, that he would never get back to Saumur and would probably be shot down by some common German corporal if he tried. He was persuaded instead, for the time being at least, to accept the invitation of the Comte de Chavigny, who put several rooms of the château at his disposal.

Later, after he had rested, Michon listened to what his officers were suggesting. He liked what he heard and accepted the plan with enthusiasm. The Commandant of the Cavalry School, with a few of his instructors and a hundred cadets, armed, motorized and ready for combat, would set off with the purpose of forcing a way through the enemy lines in order to reach the Unoccupied Zone and thereafter Montauban and the Directorate of Cavalry. They would represent, it was argued, the Cavalry School's final square of resistance.

Colonel Michon gave orders for his hundred cadets to be assembled, and Lieutenant Périn de St-André was nominated the Colonel's aide. Commandant de Launay, the mayor of Vendôme, a distinguished cavalry officer of the First World War who had put on his uniform to help the Cavalry School at a time of need, was summoned to the salon of the château, where Colonel Michon had established a temporary office. He told de Launay that he was handing over to him the command of the rest of the cadets and that he, de Launay, should conduct their surrender to the Germans when the time came. Commandant de Launay, twice decorated for valour in the First World War, protested strongly at the doleful mission he was being made to undertake. It was only after Michon had several times read to him the words in General Pichon's dispatch about saving the young élite of the Cavalry that he finally agreed. It was impossible to take everyone with him, Michon explained, as that woud mean using trucks for transport, which would reduce their chances of getting through enemy-occupied country.

Michon then wrote out his order of the day, the last he was to write for the school while it was still free. It was really an apologia for his own action, an attempt to rationalize what he intended to do. It was a strange document in which he saw himself, as Commandant of the school, as somehow personifying its spirit.

> The Colonel cannot accept [he wrote], that the spirit of the school be made prisoner. Guarded by a mobile detachment and ready for combat, he will attempt to save it. This attempt can only succeed by force. The detachment must of necessity be reduced in number. Also it is essential that those elements of the school that cannot take part in this last surge of its energy, and must as a result undergo the severe test of captivity, should maintain the sentiments of great pride for the acts of heroism accomplished these last few days. They will impress themselves upon the victor by their pride and the dignity of their bearing. They must remember that they are the body of the school and that this body is neither in a panic nor running away. They will allow themselves to be made prisoner and, despite these setbacks, maintain the undying valour of the Cavalry. They will demonstrate this valour by their order and their discipline. Commandant de Launay has sufficient magnanimity and distinction to accept the sacrifice that I impose on him and on the officers and pupils whom I have placed under his command.

The Commandant of the Cavalry School then summoned his officers into the hall of the château to say goodbye to them. 'Gentlemen,' Colonel Michon said, 'we are entirely surrounded. The school has done its duty and I am proud of you. I cannot allow a supreme sacrifice which would be useless. I am departing and I shall do my best to get through.' Commandant de Launay, he said, would surrender the school to the Germans and they, he said, as a parting headmasterly shot, must see that the pupils were impeccably dressed when the Germans arrived.

Colonel Michon's flying column had formed up and was ready to move. There were fifty motorcycles with sidecars, each equipped with an automatic weapon; there were eight small caterpillar vehicles, also armed, together with the three Hotchkiss tanks that had survived Alain Pitiot's fateful engagement at Aunis Farm. There were also four armoured cars, each with a 25 mm cannon belonging to Captain de Neuchèze's *Groupe Franc.* The Captain, in one of them, was at the head of the column. Colonel Michon rode at the centre of it, in a Peugeot car driven by de Gaillard de Lavaldène. At the last minute another of his staff officers, Lieutenant Puzenet, who had been ordered to stay behind with de Launay, came out with a little basket containing a packet of jam sandwiches for the Colonel. Seeing his colonel had no top coat for the journey, Puzenet offered him his own, with its lieutenant's insignia. Michon accepted it gratefully. 'The two stripes on the sleeve will make me feel young again,' he said with a sad smile. Handshakes, attention, military salutes and then, after a moment's hesitation about the route, they were off, taking the road to Loudun, from where they would make for Poitiers and on to Montauban in the south.

At the Château de Chavigny, after the column had gone, those cadets who had been left behind felt suddenly a sense of outrage as the realization sank in that they now faced inevitable captivity. They became angry, feeling that they had been betrayed. They all felt themselves capable of making the attempt with Colonel Michon to fight their way through to the south. What had been the point of all the fighting of the past couple of days, they were asking, if in the end they were to be ordered to surrender without further resistance? Their new commanding officer, Commandant de Launay, was not saying much. In fact, he appeared to be acting rather strangely. He had taken the order of the day, signed by Colonel Michon, and sealed it in a bottle. Now he was burying it in a corner of the park. Was it because he felt it was an historic document that ought not to fall into enemy hands, or was he getting rid of the cause of his own discontent? As it happened, the document was saved for posterity, eventually finding its way into France's military archives.

Commandant de Launay then issued an order for all arms to be handed in, and at that point all the pent-up fury of the cadets exploded. Some flatly refused to part with their rifles, others decided not to stay any longer and, with the tacit approval of their officers, disappeared over the wall of the park into the trees to make their own independent attempt, single-handed or in small groups, to escape the Germans and reach the south. But these were the few; in the end de Launay and his officers were able to calm their pupils and persuade them to submit to discipline. A sudden torrential rainstorm helped dampen their rage – and everything else in their makeshift camp, and in the morning they heard, almost with relief, that the German arrival was imminent.

Two companies of German Infantry, about 450 men, together with some horse-drawn vehicles, stopped near the entrance to the park of the château. They had not at first been aware of the presence in the area of the remnants of Colonel Michon's force and other diverse elements of the French Army who had also taken shelter in the park. But going into the baker's shop in the village, the Germans had been surprised by the abnormally large quantity of bread available for such a small village. Their suspicions aroused, they began to look around.

Now a German Infantry sergeant and two others came onto the terrace of the château, where Commandant de Launay and some of his officers were standing. 'You speak to them,' de Launay told one of his officers. 'I cannot bring myself to do it.'

The lieutenant spoke in German. 'We are the Cavalry School of Saumur,' he said. 'We have been ordered to cease fighting.'

The German sergeant said: 'That is an order you must find painful to carry out.'

De Launay, using Captain Marzolf, an Alsatian, as interpreter, then said he was ready to discuss the surrender of the school. The sergeant said he would have to return to Seuilly, about four kilometres away, to his headquarters, to place the matter in the hands of his senior officers. He asked that a French civilian might go with him to act on behalf of the school. The Comte de Chavigny offered his services and departed with the sergeant. They were not long absent.

Meanwhile some 200 men of the 7th German Panzers entered the grounds of the château, and sentries armed with machine-guns were posted at various vantage-points. For the cadets at Chavigny it was the beginning of captivity.

Before their departure de Launay obtained permission to hold a short religious service. The cadets formed up in groups behind the château. Prayers were said for those of their comrades who had died along the banks of the Loire and at

Aunis Farm. As they sang their hymns, loudly and passionately, they dispersed much of their pent-up emotion. The sound of their young voices carried into the trees, where their German captors were standing, listening to them. Commandant de Launay spoke to them; his words, too, were full of emotion as he tried to give comfort and encouragement to ardent young Frenchmen of eighteen and nineteen years of age in the hope that they might believe that France, on this dark day in its history, might still have a future. They had fought like lions, he told them. The school had done its duty; the standard had not been captured and one day it would fly proudly again at Saumur.

On Sunday 23 June, the day after General Huntziger had signed the armistice, the 300 cadets were on the road, a column of about a thousand prisoners, marching first to Chinon and then later, crossing the river, on to Bourgueil and beyond to the prison camp at Milliet in the forest, a camp built originally by the French for German prisoners.

French civilians, whom they saw along the way, seemed to be going about their Sunday business as if nothing of particular importance had been happening in their country; they seemed quite indifferent to the young soldiers being marched along the road by their German captors; the Sunday fishermen were out as usual on the Loire and did not bother to look up from their rods and lines. But when they reached Chinon, the spirits of the captive cadets rose, for here they found that a small crowd, mostly young girls, had formed to welcome them. They had prepared food for them, and this was eagerly accepted. At Avoine, the townspeople formed a long line at the edge of the road, and once again there were gifts of cheese, cider, milk and cake. Some of the women were weeping. As they went on, the march became more relaxed and even the German guards were not always paying attention – which was fortunate for Lieutenant Raymond de St-Germain, who was waiting for a chance to make his escape. In the woods before Bourgueil he suddenly slipped away into the trees, undetected, and went on to continue a distinguished military career, in due course becoming a general.

In the camp at Milliet the cadets found some of their missing comrades – Raymond Deutz d'Arragon and Bernard du Bellaing and others of Jacques Desplats' brigade who had defended the island at Gennes and been captured when their ammunition ran out. Here, too, were some of the Algerian riflemen who had been their comrades in arms at the bridges. And they were reunited with the St-Maixent infantry cadets who had been captured as their trucks had driven into Chinon. By this time, however, they had been moved back to Bourgueil, where a great multiplicity of prisoners from a variety of units and a variety of battlefields were living in conditions of some squalor. Here they were to spend five days.

One of their squadron commanders, Captain Marzolf, the Alsatian, who before the war on a visit to Germany had been introduced to Goering, was doing his best for the cadets by some skilful name-dropping. When he learned that the Germans had not themselves occupied the Cavalry School, he eventually obtained permission on behalf of Commandant de Launay for the cadets and their instructors to quit the prison camp and return to the Cavalry School, where they would be detained until it was clear what was to happen to those elements of France's forces that had been captured at the time of the signing of the armistice. To sleep in one's own bed again, to eat once more in the mess, was a welcome change after the conditions of the prison camp. At the same time, however, they found it disturbing: they were not at ease at the Cavalry School in such totally different circumstances, with only half their usual number present, and all about them the still smoking rubble of the shattered town.

Meanwhile, as at Poitiers where Colonel de Laissardière was arguing the case for the release of his horses and those officers and cadets who had been made prisoner with them, so too at Saumur itself it was being put to the German command that the staff and pupils now being held in the school ought to be released. The Cavalry School, they argued, was not a fighting unit but an educational establishment for the training of young officers for the Cavalry and the Service Corps, and it was only when the advance of the German Panzers posed a threat to the school that its Commandant had been obliged as a matter of honour to defend it with his staff and pupils.

The German command was to show considerable understanding. There was no general in the German Army better able to appreciate the courage and sacrifice of the young French cadets and the plight of those, who, having survived the battle, were now the prisoners of the victor, than General Kurt Feldt, who, commanding the 1st German Cavalry Division, had been their adversary at Saumur. Feldt's friend and fellow general, von Senger und Etterlin,* who before 1914 had been a Rhodes Scholar at Oxford, in his book *Neither Fear nor Hope* describes what had happened to Feldt just before the battle at Saumur.

'My adjutant, the son of General Feldt, drove his tracked vehicle over a mine, killing the occupants. I had taken the young officer on my staff and that day had made him follow in the rear to ensure his safety. His brother had fallen in the Polish war. It was my bitter duty to write to the father who commanded the cavalry division that he no longer had any sons. It was only three days since I had left his command area taking his son with me.'

On 2 July several German generals visited the Cavalry School at Saumur and were taken on a tour of inspection. Later the cadets learned that they were to be released, that the general in command, out of respect for their courage and sacrifice in battle, had authorized their release. Moreover, he urged them to evacuate the school as quickly as possible and cross the Demarcation Line into the Unoccupied Zone. His successor was due shortly and might well countermand the order.

The cadets and their instructors needed no encouragement to leave. They were gone the next day, 4 July, one brigade marching behind the other, making for Loches, the nearest point at which the Demarcation Line could be crossed. As they went for the last time through the streets of Saumur, where the rubble was being cleared away, the townsfolk seemed to them to be glum and melancholy, but when they recognized their young defenders, there were suddenly cheers and shouts of encouragement.

The torrid heat of June had continued into July, and the long day on the road was exhausting. A few of the marchers became distressed and were picked up and given a lift by German motorcyclists. On the first day they covered forty-three kilometres. The following day it poured with rain and they

* His son, General Dr F.M. von Senger und Etterlin jnr., in 1982 C-in-C, Allied Armies in Europe, is the author of *Die 24 Panzer Division, Vormals 1 Kavelleriedivision 1939-45* in which he describes the Division's combat at Saumur with the French Cavalry Cadets.

managed only thirty-five kilometres. There was not enough to eat or drink but despite everything their mood of elation persisted. And then on 6 July they came in sight of Loches and its great castle.

On the outskirts of the town they waited for the stragglers to catch up. Some of them looked exhausted; all were bedraggled. Several hours had now to be spent in cleaning up, in dusting off uniforms, in polishing boots. '*Soyez élégants*' – 'Be elegant' – was one of the standing rules of the school, and they were. If there was a panache about the Cavalry, that *arme d'élégance* of the French Army, then they, its cadets, were determined to show it as they marched through Loches, birthplace of the soldier poet Alfred de Vigny, author of *Servitude et grandeur militaires*, standard reading in every French military school.

The people of Loches were cheering and raising their hats as the column of Cadets came marching through the streets singing *La Madelon* as they went. As the barrier that separated Occupied France from the Free Zone opened to let them through, the Germans stood stiffly to attention. It was all very correct.

At nearby St-Cyran-du-Jambot, Madame Draque del Castillo was waiting in her great château to play hostess to the cadets. And it was here a few days later that they were visited and inspected by General Pichon, who told them that it was thanks to their defence of the Saumur sector that General Héring, with whom he had been in touch, was now safely with his Army of Paris in the Free Zone. They had, what's more, he said, done something for the honour of France.

The cadets whom General Pichon addressed at the château were, of course, only part of the original force that had gone into battle under the command of Colonel Michon. Like a Roman centurion, the Commandant of the Cavalry School had quit Lerné with a hundred of his cadets to try to make his way south. By 8 July, after a narrow escape from the Germans occupying Poitiers, where Colonel de Laissardière and his horses were being held in the artillery depot, Michon and his column reached Montauban and rejoined his second-in-command, Lieutenant-Colonel Massiet, at General Rupied's headquarters.

Some of the cadets made prisoner during the fighting, in

particular those belonging to Lieutenant Noirtin's brigade of Service Corps pupils, taken when the Germans got across the river to Petit-Puy, were moved to Germany, and many months went by before they were able to return home. And there were the cadets of Captain Foltz's squadron who had not turned up at the assembly point during the night of 20/21 June. Nor was there any news of the brigade commanded by Martin de Marolles, one of Captain de St-Blanquat's brigades that had disappeared during the fighting at Aunis Farm.

After the Germans had occupied the Château de Chavigny at Lerné, Lieutenant Lucien Fraisse, the Jesuit priest, obtained permission to return to Aunis Farm with a couple of his men, accompanied by a German escort. His mission was to try to find out what had happened to the wounded and dead and establish who was still missing. It was while he was going over the battlefield at Aunis that he was suddenly surprised to see the bedraggled, unshaven face of Martin de Marolles peering out of a cave near a disused quarry. He appeared delighted and relieved to see his fellow officer. Fraisse tried to signal to him to hide but the German NCO who was following had already seen him, and before long Martin de Marolles with some thirty cadets joined the ranks of the prisoners. They had been in hiding ever since the Germans had overrun their positions during the attack on Aunis Farm.

There was no news of Captain Foltz and his squadron, and it was presumed that they had been captured. It was to be some time before they heard that, while they themselves were the prisoners of the Germans, the cadet brigades of Captain Foltz were still fighting. After receiving Colonel Michon's order to withdraw and assemble at Roiffé at the other end of the sector, Foltz had spent several hours during the night trying to find his fellow combatants from the Cavalry School. Finally he decided that, as the Germans were well across the path that he would have to take to reach Fontevrault in the east, he would keep on south towards Argenton, hoping to link up with other French units that might still be resisting. Reaching Argenton with about a hundred men, all that remained of the 148 who originally formed his squadron, Foltz was welcomed by Colonel de Brauer of the 1st Division of Mechanized Cavalry, who was preparing to defend the town against the German advance. At Argenton

Foltz found others who had failed to reach the assembly point at Roiffé, including a cadet who had been with Desplats on the island at Gennes and had escaped captivity, and another who was a survivor of de la Lance's brigade that had defended the railway viaduct. Another was an infantry cadet from St-Maixent. All were reunited under Foltz's command.

The Germans were expected to arrive in the morning. Meanwhile the hotel at Argenton put on a splendid dinner for the cadets, who had been living on hardtack since their last meal in the mess at the Cavalry School. They sat at candle-lit tables and drank numerous toasts to the glory of the Cavalry School. There was something quite unreal about the occasion: elation and inebriation. As they stood to attention and sang the *Marseillaise*, in the night the sound of their singing carried even to the sentries at the entrance to the town.

Just before dawn those sentries signalled the approach of the German columns, and the battle began. Albert de Galbert, with his brigade on foot, made a sortie to the north of the town and fought an engagement with some thirty Germans, inflicting casualties, before pulling back with his own force intact. As usual, however, the Germans were superior in numbers and arms, and French resistance, halting them temporarily, remained little more than symbolic, the expression of a professional soldier's pride.

At three o'clock in the afternoon Colonel de Brauer ordered Foltz to pull out and make for Bressuire, a bigger town to the south. This too they would defend. The name of the place stirred memories from an heroic past familiar to every French schoolboy. Here, after the revolution of 1789, a twenty-one-year-old hero of the Royalist resistance, 'Monsieur Henri' – Henri de la Rochejacquelin – had rallied his men with the cry: 'If I advance, follow me. If I retreat, kill me. If I die, avenge me!'

Outside Bressuire a party of civilians on the road warned them not to go any further, that the Germans were already in the town. Foltz was not deterred. Going on cautiously, he found no Germans, nor was there any sign of the French troops he was supposed to relieve. Once more the cadets took up positions in front of the town. Early in the evening the first German motorcyclists arrived from Thouars, directly south from Saumur, to be met by a tremendous fusillade and forced to scatter. Once more battle was joined. As usual, German artillery batteries, out of range, bombarded the town, and aircraft flew in low to bomb from the air. It was always the same pattern. Foltz and his men held on for ninety minutes before withdrawing once more.

Meanwhile the irrepressible Lieutenant Albert de Galbert accompanied by one of his young men, Claude de Labrusse, had departed once again on a sortie against the enemy. De Labrusse, who had at one time been Foltz's secretary, had since the death at Gennes of Jacques de Frenne de Tiège become the senior cadet in de Galbert's brigade.

North of the town instructor and cadet were suddenly confronted by a German detachment consisting of two tanks and a platoon of motorcyclists, all firing as they advanced. De Galbert and de Labrusse dived for cover into an orchard at the edge of the road and lay quiet for a moment. Then, to the cadet's astonishment, he saw de Galbert, 'silent, supple, as rapid as a cat', moving under cover of a wall and chasing the German tanks. He was armed with an automatic pistol. Labrusse followed, 'calm and attentive to orders'. De Galbert was now very close to where the tanks were moving on the other side of the wall; the shutters of the tank were open, and de Galbert could make out the shape of the crewmen inside. When they were about three metres from him, he suddenly stood up, firing his pistol through the shutters and putting the crew out of action. De Labrusse meanwhile had fired on the second tank, whose shutters had slammed shut. The tank was firing in all directions, unsure of where the attack had come from. De Galbert, hit in the chest and leg, fell. De Labrusse was hit lightly above the right knee but, despite his wound, was able to pull his instructor into the shelter of a nearby house. Leaving de Galbert with its owner, Monsieur Charrier, the local hardware merchant, de Labrusse, believing his leader was about to die, went in search of a priest. He found instead one of his comrades, told him de Galbert was in a bad way, having been hit in the lungs, and asked him to get help. Captain Foltz himself arrived.

It was nine o'clock in the evening of 22 June. Although they did not know it, the armistice had been signed. Foltz had been ordered to move south again but he could muster only some seventy of his men. He was loth to leave de Galbert behind but realized that the only way the lieutenant's life could be saved was to get medical attention for him from the Germans – and quickly. While de Labrusse stayed with his instructor, Monsieur Charrier went off to find the Germans. He returned with a German officer who took note of de Galbert's condition and soon had an ambulance to pick him up. Eventually de Galbert found himself a prisoner in the hospital at La Flèche, the town where his mother lived, where he had grown up and been to school.

At the southern end of the town Captain Foltz was trying to assemble his men in the dark. Many of them were missing, so, with one of his cadets, he set off with a motorcycle and sidecar to search for them. The town seemed to be full of Germans, and it was difficult to keep out of their way. Two other cadets, similarly mounted, joined the search and were fired on and chased by the Germans. Foltz decided they could not wait any longer, and once more they took the road south, this time to Secondigny. Here again there was no sign of French troops. In the morning, just before the German advance guard reached the town, Foltz took his men into the nearby forest. He then sent Instructor Lieutenant the Comte de Parcevaux with his brigade to carry out a reconnaissance. They came back to report that the squadron – or what was left of it – was completely surrounded.

Foltz then decided that with their limited numbers and with their ammunition almost exhausted, the time had come to disband, for each man to seek his own salvation. The armistice had been signed and he did not know to whom he should address himself for new orders. It was a difficult decision for him to make. His group still looked in good condition. Captain Hachette of Colonel du Vigier's staff who had seen them at Secondigny had told Foltz: 'You're the first unit in proper order and armed that I've found. I congratulate you.' Foltz made his decision. 'It was a terribly sad moment,' he wrote later. 'In that forest I passed some of the worst hours of my life. The problems that I had to deal with. What was my duty now?'

He called the men together. It was late on the Sunday afternoon. 'We are going to break up,' he told them. 'Weapons and ammunition must be carefully buried in the forest.' He told them they had fought well, that he was proud of them; they had fulfilled their duty and now his final advice to them was to travel alone or in small groups and try to reach the Free Zone. If they succeeded in getting to Montauban, they should report to the Director of Cavalry. Some of the cadets climbed into the only vehicle they had, a Saurer truck, and departed. Others set off on foot through the trees in the direction of Poitiers. Foltz himself, with one or two others, decided to go back to Bressuire for news of de Galbert and then on again to Doué la Fontaine to find out about another of his officers, Lieutenant Bonnin, not knowing that he had already died of his wounds.

On their way back towards the Loire they were intercepted by a German patrol and made prisoners. They were held at Thouars for three days, after which, with another thousand French soldiers who also had been captured after the signing of the armistice, they were released and allowed to make their way to the Unoccupied Zone. On 6 July Foltz was reunited with his squadron at Montauban, and with fellow instructors and their cadets whom he had not seen since their departure from the Cavalry School on 18 June.

In his official report Colonel Michon wrote: 'The squadron of the heroic Captain Foltz distinguished itself brilliantly, holding off the enemy with the remnants of his unit, at Argenton-le-Château on the 21st, at Bressuire on the 22nd and on the 23rd in the forest of Secondigny, where, having no more supplies, he had his weapons buried and advised his magnificent fighters to take their chance to escape capture by the enemy.' The modest Foltz himself was to write: 'I was happy to have avoided my squadron being made prisoner. My pupils, who held together well, and among whom some turned out to be real leaders, were led by excellent officers. Myself, I did my best, using what I had learned from the last war....' Altogether his squadron received thirty-five citations or mentions in dispatches. Albert de Galbert was made an officer of the Legion of Honour, and Cadet de Frenne de Tiège was posthumously awarded the Military Medal.

There were many other awards made to the cadets of Saumur, and early in July General Réquin, who had taken over from General Huntziger when the latter had been ordered to conduct the armistice negotiations, came specially to Montauban to pin the Croix de Guerre on the uniforms of twelve officers and thirty cadets. Other awards were made later.

Not all the survivors had arrived at Montauban. The horses, and with them Colonel de Laissardière, were still being held, and it was not until 24 July that the Germans at Poitiers finally agreed to let them go. Colonel de Laissardière's determination had finally been successful. His interviews with General von Dingelleben, commanding the 6th German Division at Poitiers, had always been courteously conducted and he had been sympathetically treated. His main success, however, had been with Weingart, a Cavalry general, who knew all about de Laissardière's achievements as a champion horseman. With other senior German officers Weingart came to see the horses, and in due course the release order was issued.

At seven o'clock on the morning of Friday 26 July, the long convoy of horses was once more on the road south to the Demarcation Line. This time there were even fewer riders, since the Germans had already released some of the French soldiers who had been in the convoy when it left Saumur on 18 June. The column reached the barrier three hours later to find that senior German officers, including the chief-of-staff of the general commanding the area, had turned up to attend the formalities. On the other side of the barrier was Commandant de Launay with two other officers to welcome on behalf of the Cavalry School the return of their horses. French and German cavalry officers went through the polite ritual required by military custom for such occasions. Colonel de Laissardière thanked the German officers for the way he and his men and their horses had been treated in captivity. Then the long line of horses filed through the barrier.

At the beginning of August the horses were transferred from Chauvigny to Montauban in railway trucks. At Châteauroux the train stopped suddenly with a jerk, and France's most famous horse, the Olympic winner Taine, old and tired, slipped and broke a leg. At the next station it had to be destroyed. It was a melancholy affair, particularly for the older officers who remembered the triumph of their colleague Commandant Lesage of the *Cadre Noir* at Los Angeles in 1932, when Taine had become a world champion.

Colonel de Laissardière's mission was over. At Montauban he spoke for the last time to the cadets of the Cavalry School assembled in their ranks. 'For too long,' he said, in his final message to them, 'we have taken the easy routes, the ones that go downhill. Our young people now will have resolutely to take those that go uphill. Yesterday at Saumur you saved the honour of France; tomorrow in the posts that you will hold you will save France.' His words were to prove prophetic, for many of those who listened to him at Montauban in August 1940 were in the Army of Liberation in August 1944.

That was a thought that might have given comfort to Colonel Daniel Michon, 'Defender of Saumur June 1940', as a street sign in Saumur today describes him. As such he had won at the end of a long military career a permanent place in the military history of France. But he never knew it. What had happened to France, what had happened to the Cavalry School, its young men, instructors and cadets, had been, in the end, too much for him. At Montauban he surrendered command of the school. After that he seemed to go into a decline, feeling that everything had been lost, that life itself had no more interest for him. Within a short time he was dead – *miné de chagrin*, they said – of a broken heart.

Epilogue

The defence of their Cavalry School by the cadets of Saumur had begun after France had asked for the armistice conditions and ended with Captain Foltz and his men burying their weapons in the forest of Secondigny after the armistice had been signed. It was to be interpreted by General de Gaulle not as an heroic end to that *bataille perdue*, that lost battle that was France in June 1940, but rather as the first act of the *Résistance* after his historic appeal from London on 18 June. And for that reason he insisted that, when the time came to build the Monument to the Resistance at Mont Valérien in Paris, the Cadets of Saumur, June 1940, should be suitably commemorated there.

However, for *France Libre* – for the Free French movement whose headquarters General de Gaulle established in London, the example and the sacrifice of the young men in their teens who fought under Colonel Michon's command had more than a symbolic relevance. Many of those who survived the combat at Saumur and reached Montauban found their way eventually through Spain and Portugal to North Africa and in due course played their part in the French Armies of Liberation, two of which were led by distinguished sons of their old school, General Leclerc and General de Lattre de Tassigny.

The Germans had entered Saumur early on 21st June 1940 and, after the departure of the cadets who had been held prisoner there for a few days before their release by the German commander, continued to use the school to accommodate prisoners-of-war. However, so many of these succeeded in escaping, thanks to the courageous co-operation of the townspeople, that the school ceased to be Stalag 181 and the prisoners were moved to Germany.

During the Occupation, Saumur became an important centre for the Resistance, notably for Colonel Buckmaster's Special Operations Executive in London, who parachuted French agents into the area. It was from Saumur that Bernard Anquetil, who was the Resistance leader Colonel Rémy's radio operator, transmitted his long message to London announcing the departure from Brest of the German cruisers *Scharnhorst* and *Gneisnau*. Anquetil was eventually caught, and in 1941 he was shot by the Germans at Mont Valérien. Seven others taken from Saumur as either Resistance fighters or hostages were also shot.

Saumur had a great deal to endure. After the destruction of buildings and bridges during the battle of June 1940, it gradually emerged from the rubble to achieve some measure of order by 1944. But then it started all over again, and this time the bombardment came from the advancing Allied Armies of Liberation as they expelled the Germans – which they finally did on 30 August that year. After the war, in recognition of what Saumur had endured, the town was awarded the *Croix de Guerre* with palm, similarly to the way in which Malta was awarded the George Cross. The citation read: '[Saumur] showed itself worthy throughout the war of the heroic conduct of the Cavalry School which gives it its distinction. In taking part with great self-sacrifice in the heroic resistance of the cadets of this school in 1940, it deserves to be associated with them. Struck by numerous bombardments in 1940 and 1944 which killed a hundred people and totally destroyed 400 buildings, and, with a hundred political deportees, having paid a heavy tribute to the Resistance, its name is a symbol of French patriotism.'

The Cavalry School, reunited after the armistice at Montauban, then moved to Tarbes, well down towards the Spanish border. Here, under its new Commandant, General Méric de Bellefon, a distinguished commander of mechanized Dragoons, it resumed its activities as best it could. Once more the horses of the *Cadre Noir*, saved by Colonel de Laissardière, were put through their customary paces by another distinguished horseman, Commandant Aublet. All this, however, came to an end in November 1942 when, following the Allied landings in North Africa, the Germans occupied the whole of France. By that time, however, many of those who had had their cavalry training at Saumur were already in North Africa with

Leclerc, with de Lattre de Tassigny and with General Juin. One of Juin's officers, in command of a troop of Spahis, was Captain Albert de Galbert.

Having made a remarkable recovery from the wounds he had received when, at Bressuire on 22 June, he had fought like a latter-day 'Monsieur Henri', de Galbert had left the hospital at La Flèche and gone to the Unoccupied Zone. Then, hearing that his mother was seriously ill at La Flèche, he secretly crossed back into Occupied France to go and see her. Caught by the Germans and imprisoned in Orléans, after a while he succeeded in making a spectacular escape, scaling two high walls to do so, thus repeating the exploit of General de Lattre de Tassigny. De Galbert made his way through Spain and Portugal to Morocco and in 1944 was serving with General Juin's army in Italy. Here his daring leadership brought him not only promotion in the Order of the Legion of Honour but the award of the Distinguished Service Order by King George VI. According to the British citation, 'this magnificent leader and brilliant commander of men' during the fighting of 13/14 May 1944 '... by his determination and dash, in keeping with the highest Cavalry traditions drove towards his objectives with such élan that he broke up the enemy positions, taking over 200 prisoners and capturing a considerable quantity of valuable equipment including twelve anti-tank guns ... and was the very life and soul of the battle'.

De Galbert's fellow instructor who led the cadet brigades in June 1940 – Raymond de St-Germain, Hubert de la Lance, Jacques de Parcevaux – all commanded tank squadrons in the victorious armies of 1944, while Colonel Michon's chief-of-staff, Lemoyne, promoted colonel, commanded the 11th Regiment of tank destroyers. Captain de Neuchèze, as a lieutenant-colonel with the Free French forces was killed in the fighting in Alsace. Lieutenant Trastour, who had managed to retrieve the de Buffévent ridingstock for the family of the dead defender of Offard Island, did not survive the war; prisoner-of-war, he died in captivity. Claude de Labrusse, who had stayed with the wounded de Galbert, joined the Resistance, was caught and died in a concentration camp. Another who joined the Resistance in the Saumur area was Cadet Michel Fourcade of Lieutenant Bonnin's 24th Brigade. Betrayed, he too was caught by the Germans in June 1944 and died under torture. Lieutenant Martin de Marolles who, 'had an obsession to take part in another battle to efface the bitterness of Saumur', also had a role in the Liberation armies of 1944. And Colonel de Vigier, who became a general in Leclerc's army, was awarded a British DSO.

Among those who turned up in North Africa was one who had entered the Cavalry School as long ago as 1887; this was General Weygand himself, who, after a short spell as Minister of National Defence in the Pétain Government, then went to North Africa as France's Delegate-General. He played an important role in helping rebuild the Army but he remained a controversial and enigmatic personality. Although he was the representative of Vichy France, he could not but be aware that it was in Africa that the future armies of the Liberation would be formed under the ultimate authority of General de Gaulle, condemned to death *in absentia* by Vichy France. Inevitably Weygand was to fall between two stools as he had in June 1940, when, wearing one hat he had asked for an armistice and wearing another he had told his troops to fight on. When in November 1942 the Germans occupied the whole of France, Weygand, now back from North Africa, was arrested and imprisoned. Later he was released. In 1945, after the Liberation, he was once more arrested, this time by his own countrymen – General de Gaulle, with considerable irony, ordered General de Lattre de Tassigny, an old friend of Weygand, to make the arrest. Expecting to be put on trial like Marshal Pétain, he was however cleared of all charges and on his release settled down to write his memoirs. His son, a lieutenant-colonel, also wrote a book about him.

For the Cavalry School of Saumur Weygand's reputation remains, as ever it was, untarnished by the tragic events of 1940, and a quarter of a century after the combat at Saumur General Weygand, then ninety-eight was able to send a stirring message to the new generation of young men at the Cavalry School who, like their celebrated predecessors of twenty-five years earlier, were under training. At the time, the cadets of 1965 were awaiting the arrival of a new Commandant. Colonel Michon's old quarters in the Hôtel du Commandement were being prepared for someone whose name was already a legend at

Saumur. The new Commandant was General the Comte de Galbert. In due course he was to go on to become Governor of Les Invalides in Paris.

Every June, during his three years as Commandant, de Galbert would welcome his old pupils at Saumur. After the war the *Amicale des Cadets de Saumur et de leurs Compagnons d'Armes* had been formed, an association of those who had taken part in the combat of June 1940. And every year, before the annual Carrousel, they revisit the graves of their fallen comrades. These are mostly in the cemeteries of Dampierre, at the foot of the restored church of St-Eusèbe at Gennes, and in Saumur itself. And there are the special memorial stones to Gérard de Buffévent, Jacques Desplats, Jean-Jacques Roimarmier and those who fell at Aunis Farm, Alain Pitiot and François Gand.

Some of these memorials have been seen by Queen Elizabeth the Queen Mother during her many visits to France, and no doubt they have reminded her poignantly of the message she broadcast in French not long before the battle on the Loire began. 'A nation defended by such men, loved by such women,' she had said, 'sooner or later is bound to conquer. Such a nation is the mainstay and hope of the whole world.' If the Queen's words in 1940 had needed any justification, it was provided in ample measure, she must have felt later, by the boys made suddenly men by the advent of war on the threshold of their school in June 1940.

The annual pilgrimage to the scenes of the 1940 combat at Saumur began in 1946. The school, renamed the Cavalry and Armoured Corps School, was once again performing its traditional function. The new post-war class was named the de Buffévent Promotion, and the dead instructor's brother, a priest, led the religious service when the first post-war commemoration of the events of June 1940 was attended by the Minister of War, Monsieur Michelet and by General (later Marshal) de Lattre de Tassigny. The cadets of June 1940 who had survived the war were once more assembled in their ranks in the brilliantly lit *Cour d'Honneur* of their school. They went through the solemn ritual of the Requiem Mass; with drawn swords they saluted the memory of their fallen comrades and listened to the exalted words addressed to them by de Lattre de Tassigny. It was a moving ceremony, and the now dwindling number of cadets who come back each year to Saumur do their best to recapture the spirit of that evening.

The following year, 1947, at the time of the Carrousel, a plaque was fixed to the wall of the school to commemorate its liberation on 30 August 1944 by one of its most famous and certainly its most unusual sons. The school records show that in 1912 one George S. Patton, a Lieutenant in the United States Army, was a pupil at Saumur, having just competed in the Olympic Games at Helsinki; he returned there for a while during the First World War, when he was an instructor with the American artillery. In August 1944 General George S. Patton, commanding the American Third Army, expelled the Germans from his old *alma mater*. One of his friends at Saumur in 1912 had been Lieutenant de Lattre de Tassigny, their chief instructor was Lieutenant-Colonel Maxime Weygand, and before the invasion of Normandy in June 1944, General Patton, with his army at Hull in the north of England, had frequent meetings with another of his Saumur friends, General Leclerc, commanding the 2nd French Armoured Division.

General Patton demonstrated the special regard for horses which he had learned at Saumur in a spectacular and practical way, one which endeared him to the *Cadre Noir* in particular. Towards the end of the war, when he learned that the Russians had captured the Spanish Riding Academy of Vienna, whose famous Lipizzaner horses, he believed, were about to be transferred to Russia, he wrote a personal letter to Marshal Zukov, the Russian commander, and sent one of his officers, Captain Clement Brown, to deliver it by hand. As a result of this *démarche*, Captain Brown was able to return with the entire Vienna School and its horses. And in due course, as the *Cadre Noir* under its new Chief Equerry, Lieutenant-Colonel Margot, resumed its traditional activities in the *manège* of the Cavalry School at Saumur, so in Vienna in the post-war years Colonel Podhajsky was able to build up again the great reputation of his riding Academy. In the eyes of the *Cadre Noir*, George S. Patton's action had brought Europe's two great riding schools closer together and had shown him to be a true son of Saumur. The plaque on the wall of France's Cavalry School expresses not only its own gratitude but that of France itself for the part played in the liberation of both by the American general who had once been a pupil at Saumur.

Finally, after the war, there was one more expression of gratitude that France wished to make, and it chose to do so in a romantic place full of powerful associations, that holy of holies, the *Cour d'Honneur* of Les Invalides in Paris, where France's greatest soldier, Napoleon Bonaparte, has his magnificent tomb. Once again it is a marble plaque set among others that record the courage and sacrifice of Frenchmen in battles over the centuries. This plaque is consecrated to 'The Cadets of Saumur', who, it says, 'having fought on 19, 20 and 21 June 1940, to the extreme limits of their resources, suffering heavy losses and producing acts of heroism, inscribed in the annals of the Cavalry a page worthy of its glorious past and aroused by their bravery the tribute of their adversary.'

But it is the custodian of this place, the Governor of Les Invalides, who has the final word, since, as a twenty-eight-year-old instructor lieutenant in 1940, he himself was at the centre of these events and is part of the legend.

'The defence of the Loire,' says General de Galbert, 'could not have changed the outcome of the war since the armistice had already been asked for several days earlier. Nevertheless, every one of the cadets and their companions in arms knew that he personally had somehow been chosen by destiny to show by his conduct under fire that the spirit of sacrifice still had meaning for a soldier.'

Select Bibliography

Alphand, H., *L'Étonnement d'être: journal de 1939-1973* (Fayard, Paris, 1977)

Aron, R., *Nouveaux Grands Dossiers de l'histoire contemporaine* (Perrin, Paris, 1963)

Aublet, Lt.-Col. H., *L'École de Cavalerie de Saumur* (Éditions de Centaure, Paris, 1953)

Audouin-Le Marec, M., *Le Maine-et-Loire dans la guerre 1939-1945* (Éditions Horvath, Paris, 1987)

Bankwitz, F.C.P., *Maxime Weygand and Civil-Military Relations in Modern France* (Harvard UP, Cambridge (Mass.), 1967)

Baudouin, P., Private Diaries (Eyre and Spottiswoode, London, 1948)

Beaufre, Gen. A., *1940: The Fall of France* (Cassell, London, 1967)

Benoist-Méchin, J., *Sixty Days that Shook the West* (Jonathan Cape, London, 1963)

Bond, B., *France and Belgium, 1939-1940* (Davis-Poynter, London, 1975)

Bontoux, N., *Île de Gennes* (Privately printed, Paris, 1984)

Bouthellier, Y., *Le Drame de Vichy* (vol. 1, Plon, Paris, 1950)

Brett-Smith, E., *Hitler's Generals* (Osprey, London, 1978)

Cadogan, Sir A., *Diaries 1938-48* (Cassell, London, 1971)

Chamard, E., *Les Combats de Saumur* (Berger-Levrault, Paris, 1948)

Chapman, G., *The Collapse of France* (Cassell, London, 1968)

Collier, R., *1940: The World in Flames* (Hamish Hamilton, London, 1979)

Cooper, D., *Old Men Forget* (Hart-Davis, London, 1953)

De Gaulle, Gen. C., *Vers l'armée de métier* (Berger-Levrault, Paris, 1934)

De Gaulle, Gen. C., *The Call to Honour, 1940-42* (*War Memoirs*, vol. 1, Collins, London, 1955)

De la Laurencie, Gen. F., *L'École de Saumur* (Éditions de L'Ouest, Angers, 1935)

Druon, M., *La Dernière Brigade* (Grasset, Paris, 1946)

Durosoy, Gen. M., *Saumur* (Éditions GLD, Paris, 1964)

Ellis, Major L.F., *The War in France and Flanders 1939-40* (HMSO, London, 1953)

Farago, L., *Patton: Ordeal and Triumph* (Barker, London, 1966)

Gamelin, Gen. M., *Servir: Les Armées françaises de 1940* (3 vols., Plon, Paris, 1946)

Gilbert, M., *Finest Hour: Winston Churchill 1939-1941* (Heinemann, London, 1983)

Goutard, Col. A., *The Battle of France, 1940* (Muller, London, 1958)

Guderian, Gen. H., *Panzer Leader* (Michael Joseph, London, 1952)

Habe, H., A Thousand Shall Fall (Harrap, London, 1942)

Horne, A., *To Lose a Battle, France 1940* (Macmillan, London, 1969)

Karslake, B., *1940 The Last Act: the Story of British Forces in France after Dunkirk* (Leo Cooper, London, 1979)

Lebrun, A., *Témoignage* (Plon, Paris, 1945)

Liddell-Hart, Sir A., *History of the Second World War* (Cassell, London, 1970)

Maurois, A., *Why France Fell* (Bodley Head, London, 1941)

Milliat, R., *Le Dernier Carrousel* (Arthaud, Paris, 1943)

Nord, P. (pseud. for Col. A. Brouillard), *Le Sacrifice des Cadets de Saumur* (Librairie des Champ Elysées, Paris, 1947)

Paillat, C., *Le Désastre de 1940 : La Guerre-Eclair, 10 mai-24 juin 1940* (Robert Laffont, Paris, 1985)

Redier, A., *Les Cadets de Saumur* (Vitte, Lyons, 1944)

Rémy, Col. (pseud. for Gilbert Renault), *La Résistance a commencé le 3 Septembre 1939* (Plon, Paris, 1979)

Reynaud, P., *Au coeur de la mêlée 1930-1945* (Flammarion, Paris, 1951)

Reynaud, P., *Mémoires: venue de ma montagne* (Flammarion, Paris, 1960)

Reynaud, P., *Envers et contre tous, 1 mars 1936-16 juin 1940* (vol. II, Flammarion, Paris, 1963)

Seaton, A., *The German Army 1933-45* (Weidenfeld & Nicolson, London, 1982)

Souillot, Abbé H., *Jours héroïques: L'épopée de Gennes, 19-20 juin 1940* (Girouard & Richou, Saumur, 1947)

Spears, Gen. Sir E., *Assignment to Catastrophe* (vol. II, Heinemann, London, 1954)

Tony-Revillon, M., *Mes carnets* (Lieutier, Paris, 1945)

Von Mellentin, Gen. F.W., *Panzer Battles 1939-45* (University of Oklahoma Press, 1956)

Von Senger und Etterlin, Gen. F.M., *Neither Fear nor Hope* (Macdonald, London, 1963)

Von Senger und Etterlin jun., Gen. F.M., *Die 24 Panzer Division vormals 1 Kavallerie-Division* (Kurt Vowinckel, Neckargemünd, 1962)

Warner, P., *Panzer* (Weidenfeld & Nicolson, London, 1977)

Weygand, Gen. M., *Recalled to Service* (Heinemann, London, 1952)

Weygand, Lt.-Col. J., *The Role of General Weygand* (Eyre & Spottiswoode, London, 1948)

Williams, J., *The Ides of May* (Constable, London, 1968)

Index

Index